MOVIE NIGHTS

25 Movies to Spark Spiritual Discussions with Your Teen

MOVIE NIGHTS

25 Movies to Spark Spiritual Discussions with Your Teen

General Editor
Bob Smithouser, *Plugged In Magazine*®

TYNDALE

Tyndale House Publishers, Inc.
Wheaton, Illinois

Heritage Builders®

Movie Nights

Copyright © 2002 by Focus on the Family

All rights reserved. International copyright secured.

Focus on the Family is a registered trademark of Focus on the Family, Colorado Springs, Colorado. www.family.org

ISBN: 1-58997-083-7

Focus on the Family books are available at special quantity discounts when purchased in bulk by corporations, organizations, churches, or groups. Special imprints, messages, and excerpts can be produced to meet your needs. For more information, contact: Resource Sales Group, Focus on the Family, 8605 Explorer Drive, Colorado Springs, CO 80920; or phone (800) 932-9123.

General Editor: Bob Smithouser
Project Manager: Kathy Davis
Cover Design: Lovgren Marketing Group
Cover Photo: Getty One

Printed in the United States of America
5 6 7 8 9 / 08 07 06 05 04 03

Library of Congress Cataloging-in-Publication Data

Contents

Getting the Most out of Movie Nights

In 1999, North American theaters sold 1.5 billion movie tickets. To put that figure in perspective, the last time so many people sat in the dark munching popcorn and drinking in pop culture was in 1959. Back then we had very few entertainment options—no cable TV, no video rentals. Yet at the turn of the millennium, despite everything competing for families' attention, movies proved to be as big a draw as they were when Charlton Heston raced chariots in *Ben-Hur*. There's a huge difference, of course, between that film (subtitled *A Tale of the Christ*) and what qualifies as "Best Picture" material today. Discerning families are finding it harder to embrace what's coming out of Tinseltown. Still, record numbers of movie fans—teens in particular—flock to multiplexes and video stores every day to be amused, amazed, and aroused.

How are you handling this cinematic phenomenon in your home? If you're like many Christian parents, you may have adopted a *defensive* posture. One father recently told me he felt like a hockey goalie desperately deflecting the bad stuff. On the other hand, movies offer a liberating opportunity to be *proactive* in this area. While parents are more than justified in protecting their children from unhealthy content, movies can also offer priceless opportunities for discussion, exploring virtues, and teaching teens how to apply a biblical perspective to entertainment—which is what this book is all about.

First, film itself is a *neutral medium* and as such is not inherently good or evil. It is a tool for transmitting information. The issue then becomes, "Do the messages communicated *within* films have any real impact on individuals or society?" While the answer to this question may seem obvious to you,

1

it may not to your teen who has probably heard more than once that it's "just entertainment." So let's look at what industry insiders say:

- "Film is a powerful medium. Film is a drug. Film is a potential hallucinogen. It goes into your eye. It goes into your brain. It stimulates. And it's a dangerous thing. It can be a very subversive thing." —Oliver Stone, director of *Platoon, JFK,* and *Natural Born Killers*[1]
- "Films have a big influence on young people. You need to be responsible when choosing what to put out there." —Natalie Portman, the teen actress who portrays Padmé in *Star Wars Episodes I, II & III*[2]
- "I knew my mother loved me, but she never expressed it, so I learned about love from the movies." —*Playboy* founder Hugh Hefner, whose adult-entertainment empire includes erotic films[3]
- "The most powerful nations are not those who have bombs, but those who control the media. That's where the battle is being fought; that is how you control people's minds." —Spike Lee, the filmmaker behind *Do the Right Thing* and *Malcolm X*[4]
- "Every study that I've ever seen that's done by the networks, the [movie] studios, educational organizations, tell us over and over again that we are all influenced by the media we consume." —Michael Warren, an executive producer at Warner Bros.[5]

Obviously, industry insiders believe media have a powerful effect on audiences. But is there any real evidence that they do? Here are just a few examples that might spark some interesting discussions with your teen: A brief candy cameo in *E.T.—The Extraterrestrial* immediately sent sales of Reese's Pieces into orbit. Sales increased 65 percent after the film's release.[6] Young women's interest in karate lessons increased as much as 50 percent nationwide following the big-screen debut of *Charlie's Angels*.[7] And when Tom Cruise stood on top of a mountain and received instructions via his sunglasses in *Mission: Impossible 2*, there was a whole lot more at stake than his character's fate. Oakley sunglasses reportedly paid around $100,000 to place their product in that scene. The marketing move paid off. Oakley sales in the quarter following the release of *MI2* reached $100 million—up *39 percent* from the same quarter the previous year.[8]

At a darker level, some moviegoers have taken their love of cinema to extremes, imitating foolhardy stunts witnessed onscreen. In 1993, several young men acting out a rite of passage featured in the football movie *The*

Program lay end-to-end on the yellow lines dividing a busy highway. In separate incidents, two teens were killed, another required 11 hours of reconstructive spinal surgery, and still others were reported injured. Within days, Touchstone Pictures pulled the film, cut the scene, and reissued it to theaters. But the damage was done.

More sinister still have been headlines involving teens killing their own parents by copying—in unmistakable detail—moments from gruesome films such as *Scream* and *Natural Born Killers.* People may argue the *degree* to which cinematic violence contributed to these real-life tragedies, but the fact that movies played some role is undeniable.

Modern Parables

Why do strips of celluloid possess such power? The answer may be as simple and as timeless as the storytelling approach taken by our Lord Himself. "Jesus of Nazareth could have chosen simply to express himself in moral precepts; but like a great poet he chose the form of the parable, wonderful short stories that entertained and clothed the moral precept in an eternal form," explained Dudley Nichols, the Oscar-nominated screenwriter responsible for such classics as *Stagecoach* and *The Bells of St. Mary's,* who added, "It is not sufficient to catch a man's mind, you must also catch the imaginative faculties of his mind."[9]

Fortunately, there are *two* sides to film's inherent ability to excite. What a joy it is to encounter a compelling, well-crafted story that buoys the spirit and communicates eternal truth. Crafted properly, movies can convey distinctly moral messages that challenge viewers to live out what they've experienced.

The authors of *The Family New Media Guide* say: "We should want our children to be able to think critically about moral issues, but we should want more than that. It's equally important that they *feel* strongly about right and wrong. After all, there are many situations in life in which there is little or no time to reflect carefully, times when we have to rely on our moral instincts. One of our tasks as adults is to help children hone this 'moral sense' so that in addition to moral reasoning powers, they also acquire the proper 'gut' reaction to moral dilemmas. . . . The good and great movies of the past and present provide us with a wonderful opportunity for developing this moral sense in our children. Quality films can do what our lectures and exhortations often fail to do: that is, to create a love of virtue in young hearts. Sometimes it takes a drama to awaken a child's mind to the drama of a life well lived."[10]

Parents, you have a wonderful opportunity before you. Aside from the simple pleasure of spending time together and discussing films over a big bowl of hot-buttered popcorn, there are teachable moments in these modern parables and character studies. We have a brief window, usually when our children are between the ages of 13 and 18, to watch and discuss mature-minded movies *together*, before they're out on their own. The key is to use movies with which you feel comfortable in a controlled setting.

Don't Be Taken Captive

For good or for ill, motion pictures speak to a captive audience in a dynamic way, communicating the beliefs and agendas of the people who create them. Therefore, it's critical that films *not* be viewed passively.

In Colossians 2:8, Paul warned members of the early church, "See to it that no one takes you captive through hollow and deceptive philosophy, which depends on human tradition and the basic principles of this world rather than on Christ." Undoubtedly, teens need to be media literate. They need to develop skills and biblically based standards that will help them divide truth and error for *themselves*. By the time they leave home, they need to be fully prepared to make these choices on their own.

Universities across America have expanded their use of movies in the classroom—and not just with students majoring in film. Perhaps symptomatic of a culture continuing its shift away from words on a page in favor of images on a screen, even literature majors now learn to "read film" (usually apart from a biblical worldview). Wise parents strike first, helping young people develop a critical eye and a discerning ear at home.

Of course, some parents may feel uneasy using secular motion pictures (especially imperfect ones) as teaching tools with adolescents. In fact, they may prefer to avoid movies altogether. That's fine. For parents who sincerely believe God is leading them that way, the last thing we're out to do is pressure them to violate their consciences.

Yet other parents are not comfortable with an all-or-nothing approach to mainstream movies. Again, the apostle Paul admonished Christians to *avoid* capture through "hollow and deceptive philosophy." To use a military model, there are two ways to avoid capture. One is to stay as far away from the enemy as possible. Another is to study the enemy's strategies from a safe distance, then engage that foe so adroitly that you can defend your homestead and also ensure escape. Families seeking wisdom in the latter should find this book extremely helpful.

After years of counseling Christian moms and dads by phone, reading their letters, and speaking with them at conferences, I've reached the following conclusions about parenting styles when it comes to movies: A **legalistic** approach (dictating standards with little or no discussion) often breeds rebellion as young people bide their time, waiting for the day they can sample Hollywood's forbidden fruit. The other extreme, **permissiveness,** inevitably leads to indecent exposure as teens wander wide-eyed through the multiplex or video store with no regard for what they're consuming. The answer lies somewhere in between. That's because **teaching discernment** inspires critical thinking based on clearly defined boundaries, bonds families, and gives adolescents life skills they'll carry with them into adulthood. It's not always easy. It requires love, patience, communication, and prayer. But it is possible. And the rewards are great!

Parental Guidance

Before we get into the specific movie nights with your teen, let's address some important questions:

"Is Focus on the Family promoting these films?"

No. The mere inclusion of the specific movies in this book does not indicate a tacit endorsement of them by Focus on the Family. We're simply looking at some of Hollywood's best efforts and breaking them down for you. Since film is a powerful tool, our goal is to help you better understand and take advantage of this potent medium in a *general* sense, with an eye on the big picture. Part of the way we're doing that is by offering you some specific examples as a starting point.

By learning to deconstruct movies, young people will be able to separate wheat from chaff. They'll also learn to file away relevant movie clips just begging to be used as non-confrontational means of sharing God's word with unsaved peers. One great example is a scene from the jousting adventure *A Knight's Tale*. Despite some flaws, the film features a fabulous moment that parallels Christ's redemption of mankind. It's exactly the type of scene that gives teens an unobtrusive way to introduce the gospel.

John Wood, a professor of theology at Baylor University, says, "People are looking for some way to make sense out of life, and since the church is no longer the place where most people are finding it, movies have stepped in."[11] If that's true, savvy teens could use excerpts from secular films to their advantage as they try to reach a lost, confused world.

"How did you arrive at the 25 movies outlined here?"

The original list was actually quite a bit longer. Our team came up with a wide assortment of popular, mainstream titles, each of which had to meet the following criteria:
- It must feature thoughtful, moral themes worth exploring as a family
- It should be well-made, intelligent, and generally entertaining
- While tastes vary, it should have at least some "teen appeal"
- Negative elements must be navigable for most families and far outweighed by positive material
- No R-rated movies

From there we sought variety. Different genres appeal to different tastes. We wanted to include dramas, comedies, biographical studies, sports sagas, action/adventure stories, and romances. There's even a musical and a foreign film. Although we added a few classics for good measure, we tried to skew the balance toward films released *after* 1990 (17 of the 25). This gives the collection an up-to-date flavor, featuring performers teens already know. Tom Hanks. Jim Carrey. Bruce Willis. Drew Barrymore. Heath Ledger. In fact, it's possible that your child has already seen those stars in these very movies. But after revisiting the films as part of a Movie Night, young people will never see them the same way again.

It's worth noting that adults often invite teens to view films for their "great messages." That's meant as high praise, but to a teenager the phrase "great messages" is tantamount to being told that their blind date has a wonderful personality. The assumption is that because a movie has something of substance to say, it must not be a blast. Sure, some of the most thought-provoking films are *not* loud, special effects-filled blockbusters. Still, that doesn't mean a movie with heart must be *endured*, which is why we've selected the titles you'll find in this book. We believe the best films for family discussion are both fun to watch *and* think about, reflecting eternal truth in a dynamic way.

"Are there ways to avoid some of the 'unfortunate' content?"

We did our best to select films with a minimum of unpleasant surprises. Even so, it's rare to find a movie intended for teens and adults that doesn't have *something* unnecessary in it. Indeed, there are several ways to head off potentially offensive material. First, your VCR's remote control can be your best friend when an otherwise wholesome story tosses in an unnecessary scene or two. Skip 'em. Silence 'em. In a few cases, we've tried to let you know where to hit the fast-forward or mute button when it's feasible to do so.

Sometimes, however, that's not possible. In the case of a film like *Quiz Show*, there's no egregious scene to jump past, but disappointing language pops up unpredictably. *Television to the rescue!* Believe it or not, there are still a few words sure to get snipped when that movie airs in prime time. Scour the TV listings. If a movie we've cited for profanity is scheduled for broadcast, pop in a blank tape and record it for future use. The network will censor some of the dialogue for you. In addition to time-shifting from television, families may want to look into software designed to filter out harsh language on the tube.

MOVIE NIGHTS

In any event, it's very important to *preview* each film yourself before the appointed Movie Night. This requires extra time and energy, but it's worth it. Not only will you be better prepared to jump past material that warrants a click of the remote, but you'll also have a healthier grasp of the talking points *before* you engage your teen.

"What if I'm still not comfortable with several titles?"

That's perfectly fine. We don't expect every family to embrace all 25 of these films. Some titles may be harder to pick apart with younger teens whose cognitive skills are still developing. For that matter, you may decide that some things aren't really navigable at all for your family, but totally out of bounds. No problem. That's why we've detailed potential trouble spots in the "cautions" section. Our goal is to provide as much information as possible to help you determine whether or not a particular film will serve you well. Then it's your call.

"What should I do to prepare for our Movie Nights?"

Preview - As mentioned earlier, parents should always preview a film privately before using it in a Movie Night setting. It will help you gauge the age-appropriateness of the content, forewarn you of any questionable scenes, and give you a leg up on the discussion material. Besides, that second viewing will often reveal even more richness and give you greater insight when it comes time to share with your teen. And isn't that what the Movie Night experience is all about?

Pray - Before and after previewing the movie, mull over the content and pray about its role in the character development of your child. Should you use it at all? If so, invite God to be part of the process. Pray for wisdom and discernment in evaluating the film and using it to touch your teen in a meaningful way. It's hard for any of us to know precisely what's going on in the heart of a teenager. God knows. Ask Him to prepare your teen's heart to receive whatever spiritual truth or moral challenge awaits.

Predict - Anticipate ways the film might connect specifically with *your* teen. Will he or she be able to relate to a character's successes or failures because of a similar life experience? Is there a romantic scenario or a parent-child relationship depicted onscreen that will hit close to home? Be sensitive to how scenes or lines of dialogue could resonate in a unique way.

Protect - Think of each Movie Night as a special date between you and your teen. More than a chance to preach, it should first and foremost be an enjoyable, exclusive time shared together. You'll go to the trouble to rent a video, ice the drinks, and fix the snacks. Go a step further and protect your time together. Plan ahead to limit interruptions. Keep siblings occupied elsewhere. Let the answering machine take your calls . . . or unplug the phone altogether. Make it the sole activity for the evening so neither you nor your teen is in a hurry to wrap things up in order to do something else.

"I noticed some PG-13 movies on the list. We've been burned by PG-13 films before and are reluctant to venture into that territory. Are we overreacting?"

Not at all. Frankly, a lot of PG-13 titles have given the rating a bad name. And rightly so. Ideally, PG-13 films should be characterized by content that falls squarely between PG and R. Today far too many PG-13 titles might better be described as "almost an R." This is happening for two reasons.

First, there's a relativistic slide. When envelope-pushing films like *Scary Movie* and *South Park: Bigger, Longer & Uncut* barely escape the adults-only NC-17 and garner an R, it makes everything else seem that much tamer by comparison. What might have been considered a "low-end R" in the mid-'90s has become a "high-end PG-13" today. Same level of material, different rating.

The other impetus involves money. Box-office receipts consistently show that PG-13 movies are, on the whole, more profitable than R-rated films—particularly since 2001 when the Federal Trade Commission cracked down on the marketing of R-rated fare to that coveted group of moviegoers between the ages of 12 and 16. So filmmakers with a prospective R on their hands will trim just enough objectionable content to land in the financially fertile PG-13 category. In the industry, the term for this finagling is *ratings creep*.

Floating standards and dubious marketing moves make it clear that the PG-13 rating now serves the industry better than it serves families. What was intended to inform parents now frustrates them. That's too bad because some PG-13 movies are brimming with good stuff. For this book, we've tried to select PG-13s with a wealth of redemptive value and what many families will consider "navigable negatives"—content that's unfortunate, but probably worth wading through with older, more mature teens. If, after reading the "cautions" section of any of our PG-13 reviews, you still feel it's not a journey you want to take with your family, by all means *don't* go there.

"I'm starting late with my teens, and I'm afraid I missed my window of opportunity. Is it a waste of time to try now?"

You may glean encouragement from the 1969 movie *Marooned*. Three astronauts face certain death when a malfunction leaves them stranded in space. Ground control scrambles to organize a rescue mission. The crew's oxygen is running low. It's a race against time. Then, just as the countdown for the rescue craft nears blast-off, a violent storm covers the cape, making it impossible to launch. All appears lost until scientists realize that the eye of the storm is due to pass directly over the launch site, and if their timing is perfect, it could provide the opening they need. Sure enough, the rocket blasts through the hole to rendezvous with the crippled craft, just in the nick of time.

Obviously, the ideal time to attempt a rescue is before a storm hits. For many adults, however, the need to help young people develop critical thinking skills for processing what's playing at the local multiplex isn't acknowledged until dark clouds have already begun rolling in. Don't lose hope. While it's preferable to "train a *child* in the way he should go," a new window of opportunity could arrive in the midst of present conflict . . . *the eye of the storm*. Make no mistake; there's no foolproof formula for renewal. Each situation is different. It could be that working through one of the films outlined in this book will spark something life-changing. Regardless, with prayer, love, and sensitivity, it's never too late to reverse patterns of poor decision-making.

"My teen practically *inhales* movies. How can I offer him more in-depth guidance?"

The ultimate goal of this book is for you and your teen to become comfortable analyzing *any* movie that meets your family standard.

Toward that end, gather as much information as possible about movies that look promising. It's not enough to rely on MPAA ratings and the opinions of secular critics. Fortunately, several Web-based resources, including screenit.com and previewonline.org, specialize in dissecting the latest motion pictures for concerned parents. I'm honored to be a regular contributor to Focus on the Family's very own online movie review site at pluggedinmag.com. Updated weekly by the same staff that monitors entertainment for the ministry's award-winning *Plugged In* magazine, this free Web site features timely content analysis, as well as an archive of more than 500 film reviews.

You may also find the appendices in the back of this book helpful.

Appendix I is filled with scriptures and quotes from industry insiders that provide further study and reflection. Appendix II is a study of the structural elements of stories which will help your teen better understand the enormous power of a well-crafted tale and its origination in the gospel story.

• • •

Teens need to understand that not all preachers stand in pulpits. Not all teachers shape minds in classrooms. Not everyone with something to sell does so in a 30-second commercial. Film is a powerful tool.

In the book *All God's Children and Blue Suede Shoes: Christians and Popular Culture,* author Kenneth Myers states, "Every generation of Christians faces unique challenges. . . . The challenge of living with popular culture may well be as serious for modern Christians as persecution and plagues were for the saints of earlier centuries."[12]

There's good news in 1 John 4:4, however: "You, dear children, are from God and have overcome them, because the one who is in you is greater than the one who is in the world." God is greater than the popular culture. Take heart. By the might of the One living within you, you can confidently go on the offensive to teach your teens critical thinking skills that will last a lifetime.

—*Bob Smithouser*

THE MOVIES

Apollo 13

Rated: PG
Themes: Courage and determination in the face of adversity, teamwork, love of family, value of human life
Running Time: 2 hours, 20 minutes
Starring: Tom Hanks as Jim Lovell; Kevin Bacon as Jack Swigert; Bill Paxton as Fred Haise; Gary Sinise as Ken Mattingly; Ed Harris as Gene Kranz; Kathleen Quinlan as Marilyn Lovell
Directed by: Ron Howard

Cautions

Houston, we have some problems. While there's no nudity, unmarried Jack Swigert emerges from showering with a woman (he employs sexual innuendo early in the film as well). Moments of alcohol and tobacco use notwithstanding, the movie's biggest problem is approximately 50 profanities, including 10 s-words and more than a dozen exclamatory uses of God's name in moments of extreme tension. That's more than one might expect in a PG film. One way to avoid the inappropriate language is to record *Apollo 13* when it airs on network television, making the remaining trouble spots navigable for teens and adults.

Story Summary

Based on the real-life story of astronaut and mission commander Jim Lovell, this movie tells of the ill-fated Apollo 13 lunar mission of April 1970. The flight's misfortunes actually begin six months before the launch date when the original crew must be replaced because of the commander's illness. Even so, that bad break gives the talented backup team of Jim Lovell, Ken Mattingly, and Fred Haise a shot at their dream of following in the steps of Neil Armstrong and walking on the moon.

Lovell is a dedicated husband and father of two. On an earlier mission around the moon, the romantic Lovell even named an area of its surface after his wife. As for his children, he handles domestic disturbances with as much aplomb as he does crises in space. He remains cool when his teenage daughter shows more interest in the breakup of the Beatles than with Dad's pending mission. Lovell also calmly reassures his young son, who remains haunted by memories of a launch pad fire that claimed the lives of astronauts just two years earlier. He's tender, but tough. He's sensitive, yet doggedly determined to lead men toward a noble goal.

Just two days before liftoff, Ken Mattingly gets replaced by young hotshot Jack Swigert because the flight surgeon fears Mattingly might come down with measles in space. The odds are slim, but it's too high a risk for NASA. Mattingly battles bitterness as he watches the mission proceed without him. But to his credit, the grounded astronaut rises to the call when an all-hands rescue attempt requires his unique understanding of the vessel.

As Apollo 13 approaches the moon, an explosion in a liquid oxygen tank severely damages the command and service module, forcing the crew to abort any attempt at a lunar landing. Beyond dashing the "one small step for man, one giant leap for mankind" dreams of Lovell and his men, this puts the astronauts' lives in great danger and threatens their ability to return to earth. The crew faces freezing temperatures and asphyxiation from a buildup of carbon dioxide. Meanwhile, the ground crew scrambles to solve technical problems—including how the astronauts can get a square CO_2 filter to fit into a round hole—and bring the flyers home safely. Family members watch and wait anxiously for news of their loved ones' fates (Haise's wife is eight months pregnant).

With the men's lives in jeopardy, the U.S. Senate and House of Representatives pass resolutions asking the American people to pray. The pope is shown leading 50,000 people in prayer at the Vatican, and Jews pray at Jerusalem's Wailing Wall. The spirits of those closest to the crisis run the gamut. Some at mission control see a hopeless situation. Others refuse to accept defeat:

Man 1: . . . The parachute situation, the heat shield, the angle of the trajectory, and the typhoon are just some of the variables.

Man 2: I know what the problems are, Henry. It will be the worst disaster NASA has ever experienced.

Kranz: With all due respect, sir, I believe this is going to be our finest hour.

At last, through the courageous teamwork of Lovell, Haise, and Swigert, as well as the crackerjack ground crew led by flight director Gene Kranz (who tells his scientist-engineers, "Failure is not an option") and team-player Mattingly, the men return safely to earth. What might have been a dark day for our space program resulting in three lost lives instead becomes, as Lovell says, "a successful failure."

 ## Before You Watch

At the time of the Apollo 13 mission, just a year after the first man had walked on the moon, the public and the news media were already thinking of space travel as routine (much the way shuttle launches create little stir today). For teens more than three decades later, manned space flight has always been a reality, and going to the moon is only a brief item in their history books. Assuming that you can remember the first moon walk in 1969, share with your teen the excitement and tension that you and the rest of the world felt leading up to that event. Then ask, "What similarly dramatic event can you recall witnessing?" or "What kind of event in this day and age would evoke the same kind of response from the public? Why?"

Bible Bookmarks

Eph. 4:29, 5:19-20; Rom. 1:21, 8:28; Gen. 39; 1 Thes. 5:16-18; Matt. 6:9; 1 Jn. 5:14; Gal. 6:9; Ps. 100

Talking Points

1. Astronaut Ken Mattingly is bitterly disappointed about being scrubbed from the mission. How does he handle his disappointment? What was good about his response, and what could have been better? For more about handling hard situations with grace, read Ephesians 4:29, Romans 8:28, and the story of Joseph in Genesis 39.

2. What role, if any, did faith in God seem to play in the lives of people in the story as they dealt with the crisis? Where were various characters placing their faith?

3. As the movie illustrates, many people pray only when facing some looming disaster. Why is that such a natural human tendency? According to 1 Thessalonians 5:16-18, 1 John 5:14, and Matthew 6:9, what should the role of prayer be in our daily lives?

4. What value did the scientists and administrators at NASA in Houston seem to place on the astronauts' lives? What indications did you get of that?

5. What would you say were the keys to getting the Apollo 13 crew safely home?

6. Jim Lovell's wife, Marilyn, had a sense of foreboding about the mission from the moment her husband was assigned to it. How seriously should we take such "gut feelings"? Why? Have you ever had a sense of dread about something upcoming, and sure enough it went badly? If so, describe what happened.

7. What does this story tell you about human nature? The human spirit? Read Galatians 6:9 and discuss the value of persistence, even in the face of seemingly impossible odds.

8. Which character in the movie do you most admire? Why?

9. How would you describe the worldview of the people who made this film? What things do they believe to be true and important about life?

10. Lovell got so close to his dream of standing on the moon, yet felt unfulfilled—even though millions of people would have given anything to see the moon that close. It's sort of like the athlete who makes it to the championship game, but doesn't win. What does this say about the power of unfulfilled expectations? Read Psalm 100, Ephesians 5:19-20, and Romans 1:21, and pray with your teen for an attitude of gratitude for the things you *do* have and may take for granted.

Follow-Up Activity

If your teen and/or family is currently facing some sort of challenge, use this movie as a chance to discuss different options for dealing with it. Emphasize the need for persistence in working at it, even if prospects for success look dim.

For viewers interested in learning more about the ill-fated mission, track down a copy of the book on which the film is based, *Apollo 13: Anniversary Edition* by Jim Lovell and Jeffrey Kluger.

Just for Fun

According to a *Christianity Today* Web exclusive (posted 8/2/01), the real-life astronauts of Apollo 13 praised the film for its accuracy, with one exception—the amount of profanity floating at zero-gravity through the spacecraft. One of the men reportedly said, "We didn't talk like that. We didn't use words like that back then." That's nice to know.

—Larry Weeden

Chariots of Fire

Rated: PG
Running Time: 2 hours, 4 minutes
Themes: Serving God with our gifts vs. the pursuit of personal glory, anti-Semitism, religious faith/priorities, integrity, sportsmanship
Starring: Ian Charleson as Eric Liddell; Ben Cross as Harold Abrahams; Ian Holm as Sam Mussabini
Directed by: Hugh Hudson

Cautions

Throughout the film people are shown smoking cigarettes and cigars, as well as drinking alcohol in social settings. Fewer than ten profanities appear, all mild by American standards (Brits use the term "bloody" several times).

Story Summary

Based on a true story, *Chariots of Fire* is set in the early 1920s. It follows two British sprinters, Eric Liddell and Harold Abrahams, as they develop an intense on-track rivalry and eventually square off against heavily favored American Olympians in a quest to take their place among the world's best athletes. But their motivations for running couldn't be more different.

Liddell, born in China to Scottish missionary parents, runs to honor God and spread the gospel by demonstrating a "muscular" Christianity. His father encourages him, "Run in God's name and let the world stand back in wonder." Liddell explains to his sister, "I believe that God made me for a purpose, for [future missionary work in] China, but He also made me *fast*. And when I run, I feel His pleasure. To give that up would be to hold Him in contempt." Along the way, he uses his celebrity to attract an audience to evangelistic services in cities where he competes.

Abrahams, on the other hand, is a Jew from Lithuania who feels keenly the inherent anti-Semitism of British society. Though the English economic system has allowed his immigrant father to become wealthy and send his son to elite Cambridge University, he senses that he will never be fully accepted. He tells a friend that England is Christian and Anglo-Saxon, guarding her halls of power "with jealousy and venom." His friend replies, "So, what now? Grin and bear it?" Abrahams responds grimly, "No, Aubrey, I'm going to take them on, all of them, one by one, and run them off their feet."

The action builds toward a climax at the Paris Olympics with both men joining the British team. What begins as a classic conflict of man against man evolves into a study of inner strength as the two battle the expectations of others and must find victory in being true to their own hearts and convictions.

As they board the boat to cross into France, Liddell is shocked to learn that the qualifying heats for his 100-meter dash are scheduled for a Sunday afternoon. Reluctantly but with resolve, he decides he cannot in clear conscience compete on the Lord's Day. When he informs team officials, they are dismayed and attempt to change his mind. The impasse is resolved when a teammate slated to run in Thursday's 400-meter race offers his place to Liddell. Liddell and the officials gratefully accept. In a marvelous juxtaposition, we then see Abrahams and others competing on Sunday, while Liddell preaches in a Paris church, quoting from Isaiah 40 ("Behold, the nations are as a drop in the bucket, and are counted as the small dust in the balance. . . . All nations before him are as nothing. . . . He bringeth the princes to nothing").

Abrahams goes on to win the 100-meter race and Liddell the 400, both in record time. At the very end of the movie, we learn that

Abrahams eventually became a lawyer, journalist, and leader in the British sports establishment. Liddell, true to his calling, served as a missionary to China and died in a Japanese prison camp at the end of World War II.

In 1981, the year most moviegoers were being wowed by *Raiders of the Lost Ark, Chariots of Fire* quietly captured four Academy Awards, including Best Picture. It boasts no marquee stars. There's a noticeable absence of big-budget special effects. But for families interested in a film with heart, character, and a respect for one man's faith in God, it remains one of the most spiritually uplifting motion pictures ever made.

Before You Watch

Over dinner, lay some groundwork by asking your teen questions like these: Sports have become pretty important in our culture. Why do you think that is? What are some healthy and unhealthy desires or goals that motivate serious athletes? Have you ever heard of an athlete competing to honor God? How do you suppose the motivation of that kind of athlete differs from an athlete who is talented and successful but runs only for personal glory?

Bible Bookmarks

Ex. 20:8-11; Eph. 2:8-10; 1 Cor. 12:4-11; 1 Pet. 1:24-25; Is. 26:3, 40:15-31; Matt. 11:28-30, 16:26; Phil. 3:12-14, 4:11-13; 2 Tim. 1:7

Talking Points

1. Early in the film, Liddell's father says, "The kingdom of God is not a democracy. The Lord never seeks re-election." What do you suppose he means?

2. In their attitude toward and dealings with Abrahams, Cambridge officials seem anti-Semitic *and* hypocritical. If you could talk to them face-to-face, what would you say about their attitudes? Actual prejudice notwithstanding, do you think Abrahams may be a bit hypersensitive? Why or why not?

3. Abrahams says that he uses his victories in running as a weapon against those he considers his enemies. What are some other "weapons" people use to gain the upper hand or boost their self-esteem in everyday

life? (Examples might include hostility, sarcastic put-downs, trading on beauty, flaunting wealth, etc.)

4. As Liddell's father tells his son, "You're the proud possessor of many gifts. And it's your sacred duty to put them to good use." What are some gifts God has given you to use for His glory? Read 1 Corinthians 12:4-11, Ephesians 2:8-10, and 1 Peter 1:24-25.

5. Obsessed with winning as the way to prove he's better than others, Harold Abrahams is terrified the first time he sees Eric Liddell run, realizing Liddell could beat him. What things scare you? Why? Encourage your teen with 2 Timothy 1:7.

6. Read Exodus 20:8-11. Today, many Christians hardly think twice about working on Sunday. Eric Liddell's refusal to run represented a very different perspective. Did you feel he was being too rigid? How do you think God felt?

7. After being knocked down in a race, Liddell gets back up and perseveres without complaining or crying foul. What is significant about that? Can you think of people in the Bible who were "knocked down" but showed strength and character in the way they finished *their* races? (Jesus, Paul, Ruth, Joseph, Job, etc.)

8. Which character in the movie do you most admire? Why?

9. How would you describe the worldview of the people who made this film—the things they believe to be true and important about life?

10. What happens when Abrahams takes his eyes off of the goal to see where his competitors are? How does this illustrate the apostle Paul's point in Philippians 3:12-14?

11. When Abrahams first loses to Liddell, he's devastated and believes that any man who comes in second is a failure. How does the film portray this as an unhealthy view? Recall ways Liddell showed good sportsmanship throughout the film.

12. Abrahams tells Aubrey, "Contentment. That's your secret—contentment. I'm 24 and I've never known it. I'm forever in pursuit and I don't even know what it is I'm chasing. . . . In one hour's time I'll be out there again. I'll raise my eyes and look down that corridor, four feet wide with 10 lonely seconds to justify my whole existence." Talk about this desperate need for validation: where does it come from, where did Abrahams' come from? Do you feel the need to "justify your existence" in your own eyes or someone else's? In what way? Take comfort in the words of Philippians 4:11-13, Isaiah 26:3, and Matthew 11:28-30.

Follow-Up Activity

If you enjoyed this film's look at early Olympic pomp and circumstance, you and your teen may want to find out more about the history of the games. Here are two resources worth a look:

• "Olympics Through Time" is an informative online history of the ancient and modern games developed by the Foundation of the Hellenic World. Log on to www.fhw.gr/projects/olympics.

• Imagine getting a firsthand account of what it was like to compete in the very first modern Olympic games (1896) in Athens, Greece. Now you can with "High Hurdles and White Gloves," an article originally published in 1932 and written by American hurdler and gold medalist Thomas P. Curtis. It's available online at www.theatlantic.com/unbound/flashbks/olympic/curtis.htm.

Just for Fun

Odds are teens won't recognize any of the British actors in this film, though *Lord of the Rings* fans have definitely seen one of them before. Ian Holm (aged somewhat for his role as track coach Sam Mussabini) portrayed hobbit Bilbo Baggins in the film based on the works of J.R.R. Tolkien.

—*Larry Weeden*

The Count of Monte Cristo

Rated: PG-13
Themes: Revenge, justice, faith in God, envy, pride, friendship, timeless romantic love, perseverance
Running Time: 2 hours, 11 minutes
Starring: James Caviezel as Edmond Dantes; Guy Pearce as Fernand Mondego; Richard Harris as Faria; Dagmara Dominczyk as Mercedes
Directed by: Kevin Reynolds

Cautions

Pistols. Swordplay. Brutal whippings. A knife fight. Violence yields a number of fatalities. Two deaths are rather graphic (men run through with swords). A man puts a pistol in his mouth to commit suicide, but the gun isn't loaded. The expressions "hell," "bastard," and "damned" appear, but profanities are rare. Two discreetly handled scenes imply sex between unmarried lovers.

Story Summary

Alexandre Dumas' classic tale of romance, adventure, and revenge begins in 1815 France with Edmond Dantes (the humble, virtuous son of a peasant) and his boyhood friend Fernand Mondego (a nobleman's spoiled son, insanely jealous of Edmond) seeking medical care for the captain of their merchant ship. They risk life and limb by rowing to the isle of Elba, home of exiled French general Napoleon Bonaparte. During their brief stay, Napoleon asks the good-hearted yet naïve, Edmond to carry a letter back to France. He obliges. But after returning home, getting promoted, and reuniting with his fiancée, Mercedes, Edmond is betrayed by Mondego and several co-conspirators

27

eager to benefit by framing him for high treason. Danglars gets his post. Mondego will eventually get his girl. And Villefort, chief magistrate and son of the vocal Bonapartist who was to receive the fated letter, preserves his own political career.

Despite being an innocent pawn, Edmond is sentenced to rot in the Château d'If, a dank fortress that makes Alcatraz look like The Four Seasons. He faces his fate convinced that God is with him. But after four years, Edmond's faith wavers. He doubts any heavenly interest in his plight. That's when Faria, an aged Château d'If veteran of 11 years, tunnels through Edmond's floor in a 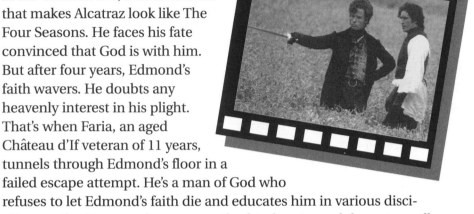 failed escape attempt. He's a man of God who refuses to let Edmond's faith die and educates him in various disciplines as the two spend years covertly chiseling toward the outer wall. Together they unravel the frame-up that cost Edmond his freedom, causing the young man to burn with anger and lust for revenge. Faria cautions and encourages him:

Faria: God said, "Vengeance is mine."

Edmond: I don't believe in God.

Faria: It doesn't matter. He believes in you.

A cave-in fatally wounds Faria. Before he breathes his last, the old man gives Edmond a treasure map and makes him promise to use the untold riches for good. Edmond also receives a means of escape. He hides in the body bag and, after being thrown over a steep cliff into the ocean, washes up on a nearby beach. There he encounters pirates who force him to engage in a knife fight with Yakapo, a member of their band who has fallen out of favor. Edmond subdues Yakapo, yet spares him. In appreciation, the stocky smuggler vows to serve Edmond for life and accompanies him to the isle of Monte Cristo in search of the treasure. The men find more gold than they can carry. Edmond uses it to adopt a new identity—the Count of Monte Cristo—and create scenarios that will bring Mondego, Danglars, and Villefort to justice.

During Edmond's imprisonment, Mercedes has married the wealthy Mondego and raised a teenage son, Albert. The marriage is loveless.

Her callous husband doesn't even try to hide his many affairs. As the Count, Edmond gains entry into their lives. He shows kindness to Mercedes and Albert while undermining Fernand's financial stability. Preying on his betrayer's long history of greed and poor judgment, Edmond ruins him. He also corners Villefort and gets him to reveal incriminating secrets in the presence of unseen witnesses. As for Danglars, his chronic dishonesty inspires Edmond to set a trap, in which the sailor gets caught trying to steal chests of gold.

While preparing these snares, Edmond is reunited with Mercedes, who sees through his regal disguise. She expresses her undying love and assures him that she only wed Mondego after 1) hearing he had been executed, and 2) learning she was pregnant with Edmond's child, Albert. Mondego refuses to take financial ruin lying down. Nor can he walk away peacefully and accept that Edmond has reclaimed what had been stolen from him: his freedom, his fiancée, his son. In a tense, climactic showdown, Mondego pridefully attacks Edmond and is killed by a defensive maneuver. With renewed faith in God, Edmond pledges to use his wealth for good and to cherish his family.

Before You Watch

Do some historical research into early 19th-century France. Who *was* Napoleon Bonaparte? What did he stand for? Why was he exiled? While not essential, this information will help teens understand the socio-political climate central to the story.

Bible Bookmarks

Matt. 12:1-13, 19:4-6; Job 5:2; Prov. 11:2-3, 14:30; Num. 32:23; Gal. 6:7-8, 6:9; Gen. 39:20–41:40; Mk. 7:20-23; 1 Cor 6:19-20, 13:4-7; 1 Pet. 1:6-7; Phil. 4:6-7; Acts 16:25-34; Ps. 73:26

Talking Points

1. In the opening scene, Edmond defies protocol to save his captain's life. Danglars believes he should be soundly reprimanded, yet their boss endorses Edmond's compassion. How do Jesus, the Pharisees, and God in Matthew 12:1-13 parallel those three characters in that scene?

2. Discuss Mondego's fatal flaws of envy (Job 5:2, Proverbs 14:30) and pride (Proverbs 11:2-3). For years, he covets what Edmond has ("You're the son of a clerk, and I'm not supposed to want to be you"). In their final confrontation, Mondego is given a chance to flee, but his ego turns him around and it costs him his life. Considering the way Mondego dies, is Edmond justified in his actions? What about his *attitude?*

3. How did Edmond's lust for revenge play out more as a bitter quest to exact "justice"? How did he show mercy to those who had wronged him, yet still make them face consequences for their evil acts? Read Numbers 32:23 and Galatians 6:7-8. Can God use people to help Him mete out justice the same way He uses them to impart charity and compassion? If so, how? What motivations might such people have?

4. Discuss the changes in Edmond's faith, from his first lashing to his exchanges with Faria to his concluding thoughts (which contain a promise to God). Contrast his crisis of faith in prison with the time Joseph spent in an Egyptian dungeon for a crime *he* didn't commit (Genesis 39:20–41:40).

5. After many years of digging, what was Faria's response when he realized he'd taken a wrong turn? What can we learn from the way he assessed his position and prepared to dig again? How did he and Edmond view the prospect of an eight-year tunneling project differently? In an impatient culture of quick fixes and short attention spans, how can we react more like Faria when faced with a long, arduous task?

6. Some teens think just being "in love" or "committed to each other" justifies sexual intimacy. Explore how this misconception led to painful consequences for both Edmond and Mercedes (He missed his son's childhood; her pregnancy forced her to wed a man who made her life miserable, etc.). Share Matthew 19:4-6 and its implications.

7. Villefort considers suicide an "easy" escape from disgrace. Why isn't it? Why should we *never* entertain thoughts of suicide (1 Corinthians 6:19-20, Acts 16:25-34, Galatians 6:9, Psalm 73:26)? See Appendix I for further discussion.

8. During Albert's toast, Edmond mentions that life's trials develop character ("What makes you a man is what you do when that storm comes"). How does this relate to 1 Peter 1:6-7 and Philippians 4:6-7?

9. After locating the treasure, Yakapo tells Edmond, "You are wealthier than any man I have ever heard of. Whatever your trouble was, it's over." People today often equate wealth with an easy life. In some ways that may be true, but what problems do rich people share with the rest

of society? How can sudden or extreme wealth actually create *new* problems?

10. Read Mark 7:20-23, then 1 Corinthians 13:4-7. Which best defines Mondego? What does he say and do that proves he values money, status, and his own selfish desires over the people close to him?

11. In the final scene, Edmond indicates the source of his greatest wealth. What is it? How, specifically, have friends and family members enriched *your* life?

 ## Follow-Up Activity

After a few days, talk about ways you could make this human story more contemporary and set in the world of teenagers (just as Jane Austen's *Emma* became *Clueless*, or *Othello* was remade into *O)*. Choose modern settings, social cliques, names, etc. You'll learn about the dynamics of your adolescent's culture while challenging your teen to relate the movie's themes to "real life."

Just for Fun

This remake is the sixth film version of the classic novel. Irish actor James O'Neill—father of famous American playwright Eugene O'Neill—starred in the title role in a silent movie from 1913.

—Bob Smithouser

Ever After

Rated: PG
Themes: Honesty, physical beauty vs. intelligence/character, integrity, sibling rivalry, forgiveness, value of humanity, female empowerment
Running Time: 1 hour, 55 minutes
Starring: Drew Barrymore as Danielle De Barbarac; Dougray Scott as Prince Henry; Anjelica Huston as Baroness Rodmilla De Ghent; Megan Dodds as Marguerite; Melanie Lynskey as Jacqueline
Directed by: Andy Tennant

Cautions

A half-dozen profanities, including exclamations of "by God" and "where in God's name," and one s-word. There's also some mild violence (thieves attack Henry and they duel; Danielle punches Marguerite in the face and uses a dagger to defend herself against Pierre Le Pieu). These minor cautions should pose no problem for mature viewers.

Story Summary

In the mid-1800s, the brothers Grimm arrive at the castle of an elderly French woman who, disturbed by the authors' version of the little cinder girl, intends to set them straight. She begins, "What is that phrase you use? Oh, yes, 'Once upon a time, there was a young girl who loved her father very much . . .'"

The young girl is eight-year-old tomboy Danielle De Barbarac, who is eagerly anticipating the arrival of her new stepmother and stepsisters. When Danielle's father dies of a heart attack, she is left in the custody of her baroness stepmother, Rodmilla De Ghent, who isn't used to getting her hands dirty and whose jealousy of the little girl is evident from the beginning.

Fast-forward 10 years. Danielle has been demoted to servant, waiting on the rude, demanding Rodmilla and her daughters, the lovely but shrill Marguerite, and Jacqueline, an average-looking girl who would be at the bottom of the De Ghent pecking order were it not for Danielle. Despite her deteriorating personal happiness, Danielle doesn't grow bitter.

When one day Danielle pelts an intruder with apples, knocking him off his stolen horse, she realizes she has pummeled the crown prince of France. Instead of punishment, she receives twenty gold coins to keep silent about his activities. With this gold, the peasant girl visits the castle disguised as nobility in order to purchase the freedom of a family servant. After an impressive discussion with her, Prince Henry pursues the mysterious young woman until she slips away.

Shackled by his role, which includes an arranged marriage to a girl from Spain, the prince drives Mom and Dad nuts, and at the end of his royal rope, the king finally relents and allows his frustrated son five days to choose a woman to marry. The scheming Rodmilla gets wind of this and eagerly begins wheedling the beautiful Marguerite into the running.

Meanwhile, through their conversations, Prince Henry is drawn to Danielle (still in disguise) and her strength, wisdom, confidence, and conviction. And Danielle realizes Henry is more human than he first appeared, treating her as an equal. A series of events draws them closer and Danielle wants to tell him who she really is, but can't.

Five days over, the big night arrives. Rodmilla locks Danielle in the cellar while she and her daughters go to the ball where the prince is to announce his engagement. Danielle appears, only to have her lowly status exposed. The prince is furious. Danielle flees the scene, leaving a glass slipper behind. The following day, Rodmilla sells her to a scoundrel named Pierre Le Pieu. The prince comes to his senses and goes to rescue Danielle, but she has already escaped. Rodmilla and Marguerite receive their comeuppance and Prince Henry and Danielle are off to pursue their mutual respect toward true love.

The Grand Dame of France concludes her great-great-grandmother's story for the brothers Grimm: "While they did live happily ever after, the point is, gentlemen, that they *lived*."

Before You Watch

Obtain a picture book of the traditional Cinderella story for you and your teen to read independently. Discuss it over dinner. Why did the prince choose Cinderella in *this* adaptation? How long did he know her? What did he know about her? What virtue was portrayed as most important for achieving happiness? Be prepared to compare your conclusions to *Ever After*.

Bible Bookmarks

Prov. 31:8-9, 10-31; 1 Cor. 13; Lk. 12:48b, 16:19-31; Ex. 22:3-6; Matt. 18:21-35; Ps. 89:14

Talking Points

1. What differences can you recall between the traditional Cinderella story and this one, starting with Danielle's excitement over having stepsisters and a stepmother? What did you like about this rendition of Cinderella? What didn't you like?

2. What qualities does Danielle find attractive in the prince? Why do you think the prince is more attracted to Danielle than to the other beautiful women who surround him? How do these standards compare with Proverbs 31:10-31? How might they apply to dating today?

3. Is the prince a better man for having Danielle in his life? Why or why not? What elements made their relationship a good one? How do they compare with the 1 Corinthians 13 description of true love and its potential for "happily ever after"?

4. Around the Gypsy campfire, Henry and Danielle discuss how people are defined by their position in society. How do we do that today? Share some examples.

5. When Danielle is exposed at the masque, is it fair for Henry to be so harsh about her deceiving him? Why or why not? How do you think that situation should have played out?

6. What do you think of how Danielle spared her stepmother's life, yet saw to it that she was punished? Do you think she forgave Rodmilla? Examine the relationship between justice and forgiveness in light of Psalm 89:14, Exodus 22:3-6 and Matthew 18:21-35.

7. Traditional versions of the story make Cinderella more passive and those around her—from mice to men—the proactive heroes. How did you feel about Danielle saving the prince by carrying him, and saving herself from Pierre Le Pieu? Would you rather that the prince had saved her? Why or why not?

8. Discuss the following quotes:

• Rodmilla says to her daughters, "Nothing is final until you're dead—even then I'm sure God negotiates." What does the Bible say about this in Luke 16:19-31?

• The queen and Danielle both say to Prince Henry, "You have been born to privilege and with that comes specific obligations." Do people in high positions really have specific obligations? Do they have higher standards for their behavior than the average person? Read Proverbs 31:8-9 and Luke 12:48b.

• The prince asks, "Do you really think there is only one perfect mate?" and Da Vinci responds, "Yes, I do." Do *you* think there is only one perfect mate for a person?

• Danielle scolds Henry, "A country's character is defined by its 'everyday rustics' as you call them. They are the legs you stand on, and that position demands respect." What does she mean? Who would qualify, as 'everyday rustics' in your world?

9. Talk about Jacqueline's change of heart. Why did she develop compassion for Danielle? Why did it take Jacqueline so long to come around? Ask teens if they know someone who takes a lot of abuse and could use a friend. Ask, "What's stopping you from being that friend?"

Follow-Up Activity

Read other fairy tales and dissect them. What are the realistic parts about them? What do you like or dislike about how the final events come to pass? Do you wish life really happened that way?

Encourage teens to write their own fairy tale. The challenge is to craft something true to human character without making it a fantasy.

Just for Fun

In the marketplace, Henry gives Marguerite a bite of chocolate. The film is set in the early to mid-1500s. While people had been drinking cocoa as a beverage for centuries, edible solid chocolate wasn't actually available until 1830 when it was developed by British chocolate makers J.S. Fry and Sons. Oops! It's one of several anachronisms in the film.

—Lissa Johnson

Fiddler on the Roof

Rated: G
Themes: The tension between tradition and social change, self-sacrifice, romantic love, accepting others, religious faith, and anti-Semitism
Running Time: 3 hours (Some families may wish to view this two-tape set on consecutive evenings)
Starring: Topol as Tevye; Norma Crane as Golde; Rosalind Harris as Tzeitel; Leonard Frey as Motel; Paul Michael Glaser as Perchik; Michele Marsh as Hodel; Neva Small as Chava; Paul Mann as Lazar Wolf
Directed by: Norman Jewison

Cautions

Celebrating the betrothal of his daughter, Tevye joins Lazar Wolf for several shots of vodka. The pair proceed to a tavern where they and other male villagers get drunk. A humorously conceived dream involves disgruntled ghosts in a graveyard. Despite its G rating, the film includes several intense moments inappropriate for young children (soldiers disrupt a wedding and later cause fatalities when they break up a demonstration).

Story Summary

In the small Russian village of Anatevka in the early 1900s, a poor milkman named Tevye struggles to maintain the Jewish traditions that give balance and order to his life in the face of challenges and change. Those challenges come primarily from the three oldest of his five daughters, who reject the time-honored system for getting a husband (an official matchmaker chooses and the father approves) in favor of selecting their own mates based on romantic love.

More change arrives in the form of state-sponsored anti-Semitism and the birthpains of the coming revolution against the czar.

As the film opens, Tevye explains that his people have a tradition for everything ("Because of our traditions, every one of us knows who he is and what God expects him to do"). Boys start Hebrew school at three and begin learning a trade at 10. Girls learn from their mothers how to be good wives and homemakers. An elderly woman named Yente arranges matches for the children when they're still young, even though the weddings won't take place for several years. In this case, she has made a match for Tevye's oldest daughter, Tzeitel, with Lazar Wolf, the elderly but wealthy village butcher. Her parents are thrilled, but Tzeitel's heart belongs to Motel, a poor tailor who has been her friend since childhood. She begs her father not to make her marry Lazar Wolf, who has been promised her hand, and Tevye finally relents. Then, pretending to have a prophetic dream, Tevye convinces his wife, Golde, that Tzeitel would be cursed if she *didn't* marry Motel.

Meanwhile, their next eldest, Hodel, falls in love with Perchik, a young university student and revolutionary from Kiev. Tevye has hired him to educate his girls, exchanging meals for lessons. On the subject of prosperity, Perchik insists that the rich are criminals and "money is the world's curse," while Tevye counters, "May the Lord smite me with it! And may I never recover!" (Early on, Tevye fantasizes about becoming well off in "If I Were a Rich Man," one of several well-known songs from the movie.) Hodel and Perchik break tradition by not asking for Tevye's *permission* to marry, but only for his *blessing*. After debating what to do, he decides to give them both.

For her part, Chava falls for an Orthodox Christian young man. They don't ask for Tevye's permission *or* his blessing. Knowing better than to think they'd get either, they elope. This time Tevye refuses to accept the violation of tradition. He asks himself, "Can I deny everything I believe in? . . . If I try to bend that far, I'll break." Torn, he disowns her.

At the same time, the czarist government is carrying out a campaign of violence against the Jews. The local constable, though a friend of Tevye's, is compelled to cause "a little trouble" for the Jews, and members of his squad break up Motel and Tzeitel's wedding reception. Then, at the conclusion of the film, the government gives all Jews three days to leave the district. They are forced to flee. As Tevye and Golde pack to leave for America, Chava and her husband make a final attempt at peace, and receive a reluctant "God be with you" from her father as they depart for Poland.

This bittersweet story, though fictional, is based on true events in Russia. *Fiddler on the Roof* (featuring classic musical numbers such as "Matchmaker," "Tradition," "Sunrise, Sunset," and "If I Were a Rich Man") was nominated for eight Academy Awards. It won two and has been dubbed by at least one critic as "the most powerful movie musical ever made."

Before You Watch

After thousands of years of human existence, despite the belief by some that mankind is improving, there's still a lot of prejudice in the world. Ask teens why they think that is, and why Jews have been a target of hate throughout history. Talk about how Christians should view the Jewish people, weighing the apostle Paul's words in Romans chapters 9-11.

Research Jews' and Christians' differing opinions on the identity of Jesus Christ. In the film, a Jewish man will remark, "Rabbi, we've been waiting for the Messiah all our lives. Wouldn't this be a good time for Him to come?" Find a book or commentary detailing Old Testament prophecies about the Messiah and how Jesus has fulfilled them.

Bible Bookmarks

Ex. 20:8-11; Prov. 23:4-5; Matt. 6:24; 1 Tim. 6:10; Rom. 9-11; Deut. 7:3-4; 1 Cor. 7; 2 Cor. 6:14-18; Job 1:6-22, 2:1-10

Talking Points

1. Like all Jewish couples in Anatevka, Tevye and Golde united by way of an arranged marriage (a practice that's still the norm in many cultures). What do you think of arranged marriages as

opposed to "falling in love" and choosing your own mate? What are the pros and cons of each approach? In today's society, what do you think is a healthy role for parents to play in the selection of a spouse?

2. Yente says, "Even the worst husband is better than no husband." Do you agree? Why or why not? Share Paul's statements about singleness and marriage in 1 Corinthians 7.

3. Tevye longs to be rich, while Perchik calls money a curse. What is an appropriate attitude toward money and wealth? Read Matthew 6:24, Proverbs 23:4-5 and 1 Timothy 6:10.

4. Which character in the movie do you most admire? Why? Discuss the symbolic significance of the fiddler, who both opens and closes the film.

5. Do you think Tevye did the right thing in giving his blessing to the marriages of Tzeitel and Hodel, even though they violated tradition? Was it right to withhold his blessing from Chava, who married outside the faith? Why? How should Christians today apply Deuteronomy 7:3-4 and 2 Corinthians 6:14-18?

6. In a conversation with God, Tevye refers to "wars, revolutions, floods, plagues—all those little things that bring people back to You." Why do people tend to turn to God in the face of calamity? What current events might be leading people to respond that way?

7. After his horse has gone lame, Tevye muses that when God is bored He asks Himself, "Let's see, what kind of mischief can I play on My friend Tevye?" Have you ever felt God was treating you unfairly? Read Job 1:6-22 and 2:1-10. How does Job's attitude differ from Tevye's?

8. Read Exodus 20:8-11 and talk about the community's respect for the Sabbath and how they show it. Ask teens which traditions in the Christian church are especially meaningful to them and why.

9. How would you describe the worldview of the people who made this film—the things they believe to be true and important about life? What does this story tell you about human nature? The human spirit? The need to adapt to a changing world and make sacrifices for the good of others?

Follow-Up Activity

Fiddler on the Roof began as a stage play before it was made into a movie, and it is still widely performed by high school, college, and professional troupes. If your teen enjoyed the film, try to find a live performance that you can attend together. Then compare the two versions.

Pick up a copy of Marvin Wilson's insightful book *Our Father Abraham*, which helps Christians better understand their Jewish roots. Or visit the Web site for Chosen People Ministries (www.chosenpeople.com), an organization of Jewish and Gentile believers who celebrate Hebrew tradition *and* Jesus as Messiah.

Just for Fun

If you think this film is too "corny," you're right. The Russian farmers are shown with freshly harvested corn, which is an American crop not grown in Russia 100 years ago. Oops!

—Larry Weeden

Galaxy Quest

Rated: PG
Themes: Good vs. evil, teamwork, restitution, the obsessive adoration of pop culture icons, how fiction can be misconstrued as fact, overcoming insensitive narcissism, refusing to accept defeat
Running Time: 1 hour, 42 minutes
Starring: Tim Allen as Jason Nesmith; Sigourney Weaver as Gwen DeMarco; Alan Rickman as Alexander Dane; Tony Shalhoub as Fred Kwan; Sam Rockwell as Guy; Daryl Mitchell as Tommy Webber; Enrico Colantoni as Mathesar; Justin Long as Brandon
Directed by: Dean Parisot

Cautions

The action violence ranges from being humorously cartoonish to more intense and realistic, on par with a *Star Trek* movie. There are about 15 profanities, mostly mild except for an abuse of God's name (hit the mute button as Nesmith begins to show frustration with a fan at the end of the autograph-signing scene). The film also includes a few subtle sexual references, some cleavage, and a scene in which Nesmith drowns his misery in alcohol.

Story Summary

The *Star Trek* phenomenon takes an affectionate ribbing at the hands of this fresh, fun action/comedy. A team of typecast early-'80s television actors—in an extreme case of mistaken identity—find themselves thrust into real-life space battle. Beleaguered aliens who have naïvely based their entire society on intercepted transmissions of the actors' cheesy science fiction series (the aliens refer to

45

them as "historical documents") land at a "Galaxy Quest" convention in search of war heroes. What they *get* are tired TV icons including a smooth-talking prima donna (Jason Nesmith), an aging beauty (Gwen DeMarco), and a bitter, classically trained actor desperate to shed signature latex headgear (Alexander Dane).

As our story begins, on-edge former stars wait to take the convention stage. They are being held up by the late arrival of Nesmith, their arrogant, insensitive "leader" whose selfish behavior continues to alienate him from his colleagues. While the emcee stalls for time, pacifying the crowd with old film clips, the crew grouses about their plight. Jason finally arrives and everyone makes their entrances. But the festive fan interaction that follows is marred when Jason overhears people mocking him and the short-lived cult hit that still feeds his fragile ego.

The next morning, Thermians from the Klatu Nebula swing by Jason's house to pick up the hungover wanna-be for what he *thinks* will be an autograph session. He's wrong, but doesn't realize how authentic the aliens are until he has already thrown the Thermians into full-scale war by flippantly ordering an attack on their arch-enemy, Sarris. Soon the entire "Galaxy Quest" crew is in deep space, unknowingly recruited to fight big, mean, scaly space Huns. And by the time reality hits, they've already reached infinity and beyond.

Evil Sarris wants the Omega 13, an enormously powerful weapon referenced in the "historical documents." No one, including Jason and his team, is exactly sure what the device does (the show was canceled before that episode could be made). Even so, that coveted piece of equipment could be the undoing of the Thermians—and the actors. In the battle to survive and defeat their reptilian enemy, the unlikely heroes encounter laser blasts, minefields, odd creatures, and a constellation of self-mocking genre clichés (Guy is terrified he's going to die first since his character wasn't important enough to have a last name).

Beyond the film's action and clever humor, poignant moments address the confusion between televised fantasy and what the aliens perceive as reality. Gwen and the others realize that sharing the truth may be more painful to their new friends than continuing on "in character" while they try to restore order. Whether hunting for a new beryllium sphere or squaring off against Sarris' soldiers, the actors must trust one another, summoning the strength and confidence of the fictional characters they're known for playing.

Eventually, the truth about the historical documents does come out, crushing the childlike faith of Mathesar. The exchange between Jason and the kind alien leader is touching. It makes an acute distinction between authenticity and fraud, addressing how entertainment can blur the line between them. The film's final showdown ends with Sarris' defeat, and the realization that all involved have matured and grown closer as a result of their unscripted adventure.

Before You Watch

Before renting *Galaxy Quest,* find an episode or two of the original *Star Trek* television series and watch them together with your teen—the cheesier the better. By seeing this material played straight, teens will more deeply appreciate the film's clever send-ups of the genre. While you're at it, talk through the plots, characters, situations, and any moral dilemmas posed in those programs.

Bible Bookmarks

Ex. 34:14; Matt. 15:14; Isa. 40:11; 1 Sam. 18; Deut. 8:2, 15; Gen. 50:20; Rom. 8:28, 12:19; 1 Cor. 12:14-20; 2 Cor. 11:2

Talking Points

1. Contrast the different leadership styles of Jason, Mathesar, and Sarris. What are the strengths and weaknesses of each? Which do you think is most effective? Why? Read Matthew 15:14, Isaiah 40:11, and Deuteronomy 8:2 and 15. Talk about "servant leadership."

2. The fact that the Thermians mistook the show "Galaxy Quest" for *real life* is humorous because it was so obviously fake. But other media creations are more subtle and intentional at creating confusion (advertising with

skewed portrayals of what's "cool," news stories with an ideological slant, etc.). Discuss some of the fuzzy lines between truth and fiction either on TV or in culture in general.

3. The same pyramid-shaped mines that disabled the Thermian ship are used later to destroy Sarris' ship. In what ways can God take things intended for our harm and use them for our benefit (Genesis 50:20, Romans 8:28)?

4. Before the adventure, Alexander loathes his haunting catch phrase, "By Grapthar's hammer . . . you shall be avenged!" Yet he affectionately calls upon it late in the film. What causes the change? Read what Romans 12:19 has to say about vengeance.

5. With which character do you most identify? Why?

6. Victory requires that each crew member—and a few fans—use their unique knowledge and skill for the benefit of the group. How does their success illustrate what Paul tried to convey in 1 Corinthians 12:14-20? Was there ever a time when you were part of a team effort like that? Explain.

7. Alexander resents constantly being upstaged by Jason. How does that jealousy manifest itself in a self-defeating way (see Saul's jealousy of David in 1 Samuel 18). Compare this to the righteous jealousy described in Exodus 34:14 and 2 Corinthians 11:2.

8. Talk about the personal epiphanies experienced by the various characters in the film. How did tensions and personality flaws improve by the end? What can we learn from those examples?

9. Guy spends an awful lot of time obsessing over his destiny, so fully convinced of his doom that it almost becomes a self-fulfilling prophecy. What are some ways in which we label ourselves "doomed" and rob ourselves of the chance to embrace life, spiritually and otherwise?

Follow-Up Activity

A day or so after viewing the film, re-ignite discussion while riding in the car or sharing a meal. Recall the costumed fanatics at the "Galaxy Quest" conventions and ask your teen why he or she thinks some people don't care that they come across as weirdos when they embrace pop culture with such abandon. Ask if your teen has ever felt like a weirdo for being a Christian. Discuss the differences between dedicating one's life to a TV series versus studying God's Word and passionately sharing spiritual truth.

Just for Fun

Who's holding the bag? Fred Kwan, but not for long. As the away team starts rolling the large beryllium sphere toward the ship, tech sergeant Kwan is seen holding a brown paper bag in his teeth. Keep watching. The bag inexplicably disappears.

Also, according to online fact emporium The Internet Movie Database, producer Mark Johnson may have named the evil Sarris after Andrew Sarris, a film critic who wasn't terribly kind to one of Johnson's earlier films.

—Mick Silva

Groundhog Day

Rated: PG
Themes: Overcoming self-centeredness, making the most of second chances, servanthood, futility in life, true love
Running Time: 1 hour, 50 minutes
Starring: Bill Murray as Phil Connors; Andie MacDowell as Rita; Chris Elliott as Larry
Directed by: Harold Ramis

 ## Cautions
Just four mild profanities pop up, but the film includes a few sexual references and dark comedic images of failed suicide attempts. To show the fullness of Phil's inner transformation, the story reveals his ugly side via crass remarks, a cheap sexual fling, unhealthy or illegal behavior, and an inappropriate gesture (counting down for the camera, he intentionally leaves his middle finger for "one"). Alcohol use is common (social drinking and drowning sorrows). A scene plays drunkenness for laughs. This comedy raises mature issues such as superficial sexuality, despair, and mortality. Best viewed by older teens and adults.

Story Summary
Punxsutawney Phil is a groundhog. Make that *the* ground-hog. Residing in Punxsutawney, Pa., he's the nation's "most famous weatherman," called upon annually to check for his shadow. Phil Connors, on the other hand, is a common TV weatherman—not that you'd know it by the way he acts. He's an insufferable egocentric. Selfish. Condescending. "A prima donna," smirks his cameraman, Larry. Phil

meets Phil in *Groundhog Day*, a clever, multi-layered comedy some families will want to watch more than once.

Under duress, cynical Phil Connors travels from Pittsburgh to Punxsutawney on assignment for WPBH to cover the town's Groundhog Day festivities. It's a fluff piece and Phil knows it. It grates on him that his life has been reduced to this. Then again, pretty much *everything* grates on Phil. So he takes out his frustration on the people around him. Accompanied by Larry and a fun-loving new producer named Rita, he doesn't even try to mask his sarcasm as he races through the gig and heads home, away from the small-town "hicks" he holds in contempt. But a blizzard blocks his retreat, forcing the crew back to Punxsutawney.

The next morning at 6:00 A.M., Phil is awakened by a clock radio playing Sonny and Cher's "I Got You Babe"—again. He proceeds to relive Groundhog Day all over again. And again. And again. Caught in a bizarre time warp, Phil repeatedly finds himself waking up to February 2. He encounters the same people in the same places. They greet him in the same manner. What's really strange is that he can remember these previous days in vivid detail, but everyone around him seems to be coasting through Groundhog Day for the first time. First he's perplexed, then frightened, then invigorated by a pair of drunks he meets at a bowling alley:

Phil: "Let me ask you guys a question. What if there were no tomorrow?"

Gus: "No tomorrow? That would mean there'd be no consequences. There would be no hangovers. We could do whatever we wanted!"

Phil: "That's true. We could do whatever we want. . . . I'm not gonna live by their rules anymore."

The self-centered, newly liberated meteorologist takes advantage of his powerful position. He plays chicken with an oncoming train. He leads police on a high-speed chase. He woos (and sleeps with) townswomen. He robs a bank. He slugs an annoying insurance salesman. Nothing matters, because tomorrow is always today. Everything starts over from scratch. No one remembers but him. Weeks and months go by as Phil indulges every carnal whim that flits through his mind. Then despair sets in.

Seeing the futility of this existence, Phil sets his mind to suicide. But not even death can silence the 6:00 A.M. chorus of "I Got You Babe" that rouses him each morning, announcing a repeat of February 2. He steps in front of truck. He electrocutes himself. He drives over a cliff. He jumps off a tall building. Nothing works. Despair turns to desperation. Then, after being repeatedly rebuffed by Rita (the one woman he respects and has been unable to manipulate into bed), he hits rock bottom and realizes that satisfaction lies not in changing his environment or the people in it, but changing *himself.*

Phil's desperation leads to hope. Rita's kind heart inspires him. He realizes he's been "chasing after the wind" (Ecclesiastes 1-2) and focuses his attention on the needs of others. He works to better himself and begins practicing random acts of kindness. He tries to keep a homeless man from dying on the street. He saves the mayor (played by Bill Murray's real-life brother) from choking. He repairs flat tires and rescues a boy falling out of a tree. He patches up a young couple's relationship. Most importantly, his selfish attempts to woo Rita turn into genuine attraction and love. He starts to care. It is caring and *selflessness* that bring an end to his inexplicable "curse."

Before You Watch

Take the family on a fun outing. Don't let the kids in on the gag, but the very next day do exactly the same thing, pretending you didn't do it the day before. Have fun with it. This will prepare teens to empathize with Phil as you watch the movie.

Look into the history of the holiday. When did Groundhog Day originate? Why? Web sites such as www.groundhog.org and www.punxsutawneyphil.com provide avenues to learn more about this lighthearted tradition.

Bible Bookmarks

Jas. 2:14-26; Matt. 25; Eccles. 1-2; Luke 10:25-37; Is. 55:8-11; Rom. 12:3-5; Prov. 18:1; Phil. 2:3-7; Acts 16:25-34; 1 Cor. 6:19-20; Ps. 27:14

Talking Points

1. In the beginning of the movie, Phil's arrogance alienates his coworkers. Do you know anyone who acts like that? How does it make you feel? Do *you* ever act like that? Read Romans 12:3-5 and Proverbs 18:1. How *should* we behave (Philippians 2:3-7)?

2. Phil's friends think he's just full of himself, but a closer look reveals hidden insecurities and fears. Discuss how such inner turmoil can create boastful, mean people, and that bullies and braggarts are often just covering up their own pain and disappointment. How are Christians uniquely equipped to offer them hope?

3. At first, Phil uses his newfound power to hurt, use, and humiliate people. Have you ever used a newly discovered talent or ability to take advantage of a sibling or friend? How has it affected your relationship with him or her?

4. Many people, at some point in their lives, are tempted to spice things up with dangerous or even immoral behavior. How does Phil prove that the best cure for monotony is turning our eyes *away* from selfish desires? Imagine how it would feel to be a full-time good Samaritan as described in Luke 10:25-37. What ways could you use that freedom to share the love of Christ? What's stopping you?

5. What's the significance of the "reformed" Phil asking Larry what he thinks about moving the camera? Explain how we can validate people and make them feel good simply by seeking their opinions.

6. Death isn't a solution for Phil. He keeps waking up again. But while suicide appears here in a darkly humorous context, it's a very serious, very final act. Talk about it with your teen. Why should suicide never be an option, especially for a Christ follower? Read Acts 16:25-34, 1 Corinthians 6:19-20, and Psalm 27:14. (See Appendix I for further discussion.)

7. Phil finds his way out of the maze by doing good, by helping his fellow man, by being selfless, and by discovering true love. What does the Bible teach about how we can find our way out of the maze of sin? Is doing good enough? Talk through James 2:14-26 and Matthew 25 to determine the healthy balance between God's grace and those works that show the fruit of our faith.

8. Phil asks Rita to describe her "perfect man." What do you think of the qualities she values? How do they measure up to godly virtues? Also, when you get right down to it, at the end of the movie Rita is fully sold on Phil after only *one day* in *her* life. Is it believable that she could know someone that well in such a short period of time? Why or why not?

9. Discuss how you might live your life differently if nothing you did effected any permanent change. Take comfort from the promise in Isaiah 55:8-11.

Follow-Up Activity

Be on the lookout for news stories about common people who make a difference simply by making themselves available to their fellow man. Read them across the dinner table.

Gather your family and brainstorm ways you can serve others *together* (volunteering at a soup kitchen, cleaning the church, collecting gloves for the homeless, etc.).

Just for Fun

Groundhog Day in Punxsutawney used to be a fairly modest event. But ever since this movie was released in 1993, record crowds as large as 30,000 have gathered each year to celebrate at Gobbler's Knob. Who says movies don't impact people's attitudes and behavior?

—Steven Isaac

Hoosiers

Rated: PG
Themes: Making the most of life's second chances, teamwork, self-control, discipline, sobriety
Running Time: 1 hour, 54 minutes
Starring: Gene Hackman as Norman Dale; Barbara Hershey as Myra Fleener; Dennis Hopper as Wilbur "Shooter" Flatch; Sheb Wooley as Cletus
Directed by: David Anspaugh

Cautions

Eight profanities (mostly mild, but there's one s-word and two inappropriate uses of Christ's name). Most families will find this film appropriate for teens of all ages.

Story Summary

It's harvest time in Hickory, Ind., 1951. Cool autumn breezes caress red-orange leaves as they scamper across the dirt roads of forgotten Americana. That's when newly hired high school basketball coach Norman Dale pulls into the sleepy little town for his last stop on the road to personal redemption. It's a notch down from the college position he held 12 years earlier, taken from him after an unfortunate loss of temper. Dale wants to put the past behind him. Armed with a second chance and a handful of unmotivated farmboys, he overcomes numerous obstacles and builds a state champion.

Hickory epitomizes pre-Elvis, Midwestern agrarianism. There's not much to do but work the fields, attend school, or hang out at the local barber shop talking about the one thing other than religion that galvanizes this tiny community—high school basketball. And everyone has an opinion about how Dale should do his job. The way he runs practices. His style of defense. Conventional wisdom also says he can't win without Jimmy Chipwood, a brooding superstar caught between the pressure to play and the pressure *not to* by the school's pretty vice principal, Myra Fleener, who believes he's meant for greater things which he might never experience if he becomes a local hero on the hardwood:

Myra: Leave him alone, alright? He's a real special kid and I have high hopes for him. I think if he works really hard he can get an academic scholarship to Wabash College and get out of this place.

Dale: Why, do you have something against this place?

Myra: For him, yes I do. He could do better.

Dale: You know, if Jimmy's as good as everybody says he is, I would've thought a basketball scholarship would have made a lot of sense.

Myra: Who would ever see him play? The only thing that ever comes through Hickory from the outside is a train, and it's here for about five minutes. . . . A basketball hero around here is treated like a god. How can he ever find out what he can really do? I don't want this to be the high point of his life. I've seen them—the real sad ones. They sit around the rest of their lives talking about the glory days when they were 17 years old.

Dale: You know, most people would kill to be treated like a god, just for a few moments.

Myra: Gods come pretty cheap nowadays, don't they? You become one by putting a leather ball in an iron hoop. And I hate to tell you this, Mr. Dale, but it's only a game.

While Dale is busy breaking and rebuilding his undisciplined team, the boys grow to respect him. His stock within the community plummets, however, due to his unorthodox style. He becomes even more unpopular when he tries to rehabilitate one boy's alcoholic dad by making him an assistant coach. Dennis Hopper earned an Oscar nomination for his role as the hard-drinking Shooter Flatch, an enthusiastic encyclopedia of local hoops minutiae who loves his son very much, but just can't stay off the bottle. He gets a hearty dose of tough love from Dale. There's a wonderful moment when Dale argues with a referee and covertly asks to be thrown out of the game so that Shooter must shoulder the coaching responsibility in his stead.

Dale's popularity continues to dip. Locals gather to vote on whether or not he should be removed from his position. The majority want him out. That is, until Jimmy steps in and says he's ready to play ball—but only for Dale. The team starts winning. Crusty attitudes soften. In fact, even Dale's initially antagonistic relationship with Myra transforms into one of mutual respect and modest romance. Like so many great sports movies, this one concludes with a climactic battle evoking comparisons to David's classic "mano a mano" with a heavily favored Philistine (the underdog Huskers are loosely based on the actual 1954 Indiana state champions, the Milan Indians). With fine performances, postcard-like snapshots of a fading middle-America, and great basketball, *Hoosiers* scores on many levels.

Before You Watch

Invite teens to share what they believe are the qualities of a good coach. If they play sports, discuss specific examples from their own experience. How did different coaches' attitudes make them feel?

Research how much we have learned about alcoholism over the past 50 years, and how that has affected the way we treat it in our culture. You may want to read Proverbs 23:29-35, Galatians 5:21, Ephesians 5:18, and Isaiah 28:7-8 for a biblical perspective on drunkenness.

Bible Bookmarks

Rom. 12:3-5; Gal. 5:21; 1 Cor. 9:24-27, 12:17-20; Prov. 14:17; Eph. 4:26-27 & 31, 6:11-18; Acts 9:1-19

Talking Points

1. After being told that every young athlete dreams of being exalted, what did Myra mean by her response, "Gods come pretty cheap nowadays"? Would you agree?

2. How do you feel about the portrayal of Christianity in the film, specifically as it is reflected in the born-again ballplayer and his father? Why do you think it's so rare to see that in today's Hollywood films?

3. Read 1 Corinthians 12:17-20 and Romans 12:3-5. How do these biblical truths play out in Dale's attempt to build his players' unity and confidence?

4. Talk about the disrespect shown to the new coach when he enters the gym for the first time. We see one boy humbly repent, at which time he is restored to a right relationship. How are his exit and return similar to man's relationship with God? Examine Saul's second chance in Acts 9:1-19 and how he made the most of it.

5. Early on, the boys just wanted to shoot hoops in practice. Dale redirected them to the basics, which weren't nearly as much fun, but prepared them more completely for what lay ahead. What fundamentals are necessary for the Christian life? Introduce Ephesians 6:11-18 and 1 Corinthians 9:24-27.

6. Dale had been a highly respected college coach until a momentary loss of self-control ruined his reputation. Could Proverbs 14:17 and Ephesians 4:26-27 & 31 have spared him that pain and embarrassment? Also, the players lashed out violently at times in defense of their coach and one another. Was that behavior justified? What is a better way to deal with anger?

7. Dale urges his guys, "Most important, don't get caught up in thinking about winning or losing this game. If you put your effort and concentration into playing to your potential, to be the best that you can be, I don't care what the scoreboard says, in my book we're gonna be winners!" Do you agree? How does our society echo that standard—or not?

8. Talk about Shooter's relationship with his son as it changed throughout the movie. How does Coach Dale's determination to believe in Shooter rub off on the boy? Ask your teen to think of someone in his/her life (at home, in school, at work, at church, etc.) who could use that dose of self-confidence. Ask, "Could you be a Coach Dale to that person?"

9. Sometimes parents can act toward adolescents like the men in the barber shop did toward Dale, wanting to "help," yet alienating that person in the process. If you dare, ask your teen, "Have I ever made you feel like the coach felt in that scene?" Do you trust your teen to do his or her job? Is your criticism delivered tactfully and lovingly? Or do you lord over

his or her every move? If you're prepared to get an honest answer and avoid defensiveness, this could inspire a meaningful discussion.

Follow-Up Activity

Plan a "date night" with your teen built around attending a high school basketball game. No object lessons. No moral objectives. Don't go into it with any agenda or expectations other than sharing a fun night out, just the two of you.

Just for Fun

Check out the blackboard in the locker room before the final game. The list of names presented as members of the opposing team are actually the last names of the actors who portray the Hickory players.

—Bob Smithouser

It's a Wonderful Life

Not Rated
Themes: Selflessness, value of family and community, integrity, making a difference in the world
Running Time: 2 hours, 11 minutes
Starring: James Stewart as George Bailey; Donna Reed as Mary; Lionel Barrymore as Mr. Potter; Henry Travers as Clarence; Thomas Mitchell as Uncle Billy
Directed by: Frank Capra

Cautions

Occasional alcohol use, some drunkenness. George contemplates suicide. The theology of angels is skewed, implying that angels are former humans working to earn their wings in the afterlife.

Story Summary

This holiday favorite begins with heartfelt prayers rising from the tiny town of Bedford Falls, each asking God to come to the aid of George Bailey. In response, the heavenly hosts summon Clarence, a guardian angel who has yet to earn his wings. He's apprised of the situation during a celestial briefing that features snapshots from George's life. Thus, we see a young boy save his brother's life. He later prevents the local pharmacist from making a deadly mistake. Most of all, we learn that George has a dream to get out of Bedford Falls and travel to big cities, build big buildings, and see the world. His father, Peter, owns a humble building and loan company that helps families and small businesses. George respects his dad's job, but has no desire to follow in his footsteps.

At first it appears that George will fulfill his dream. Then, on the night before he's scheduled to leave for college, his father suffers a fatal stroke. As executor of the estate, George must address the future of the family business, which will be shut down if greedy board member Mr. Potter has his way. The board votes to keep the doors open on one condition: George Bailey must step into his father's shoes and run the company. George is trapped. If he follows his own star, years of community vision and service will end. But if George continues his father's work, he'll lose his chance to see the world.

Several years pass. George watches as his brother and best friends leave town to pursue their dreams. Meanwhile, he falls in love with a sweet girl named Mary, and they have grand honeymoon plans. But on their wedding day, there's a run on the banks. George and Mary sacrifice their entire honeymoon fund to keep the building and loan afloat, preserving the one institution helping local folks to escape the grip of Potter, the callous slumlord who controls the town's rental property. It takes some creativity, but these people are hard workers who just need a break. The Baileys give them that break.

Of course, George never loses sight of his dream, and one day opportunity knocks in the most unexpected way. Mr. Potter offers George a high-paying job with a chance to travel. It's too good to be true. "What about the building and loan?" George asks. Realizing that Potter is spinning a web of deceit, he quickly walks away from the opportunity of a lifetime.

As Clarence is briefed on George's life, he learns of the event that triggered the prayers of family and friends. George's brother is coming home to a war hero's welcome. In his excitement, Uncle Billy loses a deposit of $8,000. Mr. Potter discovers the money and keeps it, seeing this as his big chance to ruin George and take over his business. The bank examiner shows up to review the building and loan's books. George knows he's headed to jail unless he can account for the missing cash and, after unleashing his frustration on those around him, goes to Potter for help. George begs for a loan, but his only collateral is a $15,000 life insurance policy with cash equity of $500. "Why, you're worth more dead than alive," sneers Potter. Taking the old man's words to heart, George staggers onto a bridge on a bitterly cold Christmas Eve, ready to plunge to his death in the icy river in order to save his family.

This is where Clarence steps in. His mission? Convince George Bailey that his life has inestimable value, and that the world would have been a poorer place had he never been born. In a twist worthy of *The Twilight Zone*, George visits a version of his home town that has never known him or his influence. No matter how many times you've watched the ending of this five-time Oscar nominee, have a Kleenex handy for the finale when the whole town rallies around George, who realizes that he does indeed have a wonderful life.

Before You Watch

Casually invite teens to talk about their plans and dreams. Be careful not to pass judgment on the merits or practicality of those aspirations. Talk about your own dreams when you were younger and whether or not they turned out exactly as planned (if not, how has God blessed you in different, unexpected ways?).

Bible Bookmarks

Matt. 5:7, 16:24-26; Col. 3:12; Prov. 11:3; Ps. 100:4; Jn. 15:13; Lk. 12:16-21; Eph. 5:18

Talking Points

1. It may be hard to read, but the framed statement beneath the picture of George's father states, "All you can take with you is that which you gave away." Is that true? Why or why not?

2. George's rescue of Harry epitomizes his lifelong attitude of putting others ahead of himself. How does he, through giving sacrificially to the people around him, ultimately find joy and satisfaction? How does this principle manifest itself in the pages of Scripture? Read John 15:13 and Matthew 16:24-26.

3. Mr. Potter growls to Peter, "Have you put any real pressure on these people of yours to *pay* those mortgages? . . . Are you running a business or a charity ward?" How is he like the rich man in Luke 12:16-21? How does Potter differ from the Baileys in the area of mercy and compassion? Based on Matthew 5:7 and Colossians 3:12, how should we act?

4. Consider the movie's lax attitudes toward cigarettes and drunkenness. What has our culture learned about their dangers since this film was made in 1946? Read Ephesians 5:18 for a biblical take on sobriety.

5. Examine how Mr. Potter tries to tempt George into betraying his conscience. How can Satan make similarly seductive offers to Christians in an attempt to lure us away from our first love, God's best for us, and our high calling?

6. Look up the word "integrity" in a dictionary and read Proverbs 11:3. How much of a role did integrity play in George's popularity with his neighbors? How can one become a person of integrity?

7. How did George treat everyone after the $8,000 was lost? How could he have handled that crisis better?

8. What did George Bailey really want in life—travel, money, grand accomplishments? If so, why did he turn down Mr. Potter's offer?

9. Just hours after complaining about living in an icebox, George rejoices, "Look at this wonderful old drafty house!" Clearly, contentment and joy are a matter of perspective. Urge teens to think of something that frustrates them and help them to see the blessing behind it. For example, many of us complain that our Internet access is too slow, yet think of how many people don't have a computer at all. Read Psalm 100:4 and take a moment to do what it says.

10. After more than 50 years, this movie continues to be a favorite, especially during the Christmas season. Why do you think it's so popular? Together, talk about how it made *you* feel.

11. Clarence says, "One man's life touches so many others, when he's not there it leaves an awfully big hole." Ask teens to ponder how the world might be different without their contribution. What can we do to make sure we will be missed? How can we make an eternal impact for Jesus?

 ## Follow-Up Activity

Appendix II of this book details the elements of story by using *It's a Wonderful Life* as the model. Give your Movie

Night discussion a few days to sink in. Then take 30 minutes or so to share that material.

In the movie, angels are used to propel the story but aren't always portrayed in ways consistent with biblical teaching. For a more accurate understanding of these very real heavenly messengers, pick up Dr. Billy Graham's excellent book *Angels: God's Secret Agents*. It examines where angels came from, who they are, and what they do, all in a readable format that could lead to a whole series of family Bible studies.

Just for Fun

The creators of Focus on the Family's children's radio drama *Adventures in Odyssey* loved this movie so much that they paid tribute by naming members of the Barclay family after people in *It's a Wonderful Life*. The Barclay parents are named George and Mary (just like the Baileys), and their children are Jimmy and Donna, named for Jimmy Stewart and Donna Reed, the actors who played George and Mary Bailey in the film.

—Al Janssen

A Knight's Tale

Rated: PG-13
Themes: Nobility of birth vs. noble character, redemption, mercy, friendship, honesty, sportsmanship, bravery, the father-son bond, the consequences of gambling
Running Time: 1 hour, 34 minutes
Starring: Heath Ledger as William Thatcher; Rufus Sewell as Count Adhemar; Shannon Sossamon as Jocelyn; Paul Bettany as Geoffrey Chaucer; Mark Addy as Roland; Alan Tudyk as Wat
Directed by: Brian Helgeland

Cautions

Fewer than ten profanities. Twice Chaucer is shown naked (rear and side) after having lost his clothes gambling, though the nudity is not sexualized. One of Jocelyn's dresses reveals cleavage. Alcohol is consumed at a pub. There's an implied sexual encounter between the romantic leads—a disappointment, but one that parents should be able to turn to their advantage during discussion time. Most of the modern music infused into the film is fine, but hit the stop or mute button just as the final scene fades into the end credits and the bawdy lyrics to AC/DC's "You Shook Me All Night Long." Best viewed with older teens.

Story Summary

Arena rock meets 14th-century Europe in this breezy, off-beat blend of *Rocky, Grease,* and *Robin Hood.* As the film opens, a trio of squires try in vain to rouse their liege, an aging knight who has passed away mid-tournament. With victory so close—and their stomachs so empty—they suit up one of their own who poses as their master and proceeds to win first prize. Trouble is, William Thatcher is a peasant. Only men of noble birth can compete. And once William has tasted competition, he wants more. He convinces his partners Roland and Wat to join him in a grand deception. Together they will tour the jousting circuit and make their fortune as William fulfills his boyhood dream of knighthood by masquerading as a nobleman.

Roland: You're not of noble birth!

William: So we lie. How did the nobles become noble in the first place, huh? They took it at the tip of a sword. I'll do it with a lance.

Wat: A blunted lance.

William: No matter, Wat, a man *can* change his stars. And I won't spend the rest of my life as nothing.

Some training follows, then it's off to their first true test. On the road, William (aka Sir Ulrich von Lichtenstein of Gelderland) and his squires encounter Geoff Chaucer. Yes, *that* Chaucer. He's filthy and naked, the result of a gambling problem that has cost him the clothes off his back. He offers to forge the medieval equivalent of a birth certificate for William, proof of nobility needed at check-in, and becomes the team's herald. Chaucer is yet another endearing comic sidekick, an anachronistic cross between William Shakespeare and the pro wrestling announcer who bellows, "Let's get ready to rummmble!" They also meet a feisty female blacksmith who rounds out William's lance-handling, armor-repairing pit crew.

A fair maiden named Jocelyn catches William's eye. Unfortunately, she also turns the head of Count Adhemar, the dastardly black knight, military leader, and jousting grand champion who quickly becomes William's nemesis. As Jocelyn's affection for William intensifies, so does Adhemar's animosity toward him. A showdown is inevitable. But Adhemar gets called away to battle, leaving William to rack up victories, woo Jocelyn, and reunite with his blind father in the evil knight's absence. Before the two rivals can go mano a mano, the seething Adhemar learns of William's fraud and exposes him, eventually leading to an excellent (if unintentional) cinematic parallel of Christ's redemption of mankind.

The jig is up. Authorities are closing in. William's friends urge him to flee, but the young man nobly refuses to run from the consequences of his sin. He is arrested, mocked by his accuser, and put in a pillory to face public ridicule. Guilty as charged. No chance of escape. Then the one man with the authority to pardon him steps out of the crowd. It's the heir to the throne of England. Based on an earlier encounter with William, the prince sees fit to wipe the slate clean, and goes a step further by bestowing on him a title of nobility contestable by no man. This allows William to battle—and defeat—Adhemar legitimately.

What a terrific illustration of Jesus' intervention on our behalf. Unable to escape sin, we all face judgment and humiliation at the hand of our accuser, Satan. There's no escape apart from a royal pardon by the only One with the authority to release us and dub us holy, Jesus Christ. It is because of our previous relationship with the King of kings that, at the time of judgment, He will step forth and intercede. And Christ's uncontestable decree allows us to legitimately defeat death.

Before You Watch

Attend a Renaissance festival or do a little research on that period. The more teens know about the actual music and dress of 14th-century England, the better they'll appreciate how the filmmakers infused modern elements to create a quirky clash of pop cultures.

Since the Chaucer character is loosely based on the famous author of *The Canterbury Tales* (a work read in many high school literature classes), familiarize yourself with the real poet and his well-known work.

Bible Bookmarks

Matt. 5:7, 9:9-13, 28:18; Isa. 5:20, 55:6-7; Prov. 3:5-6, 17:17; Jn. 15:13; 1 Cor. 2:10-16, 6:18-20; 2 Cor. 5:16-19; Heb. 13:4; 1 Thes. 4:3-5; Rom. 5:6-11, 6:23; 1 Pet. 2:9-10; Rev. 12:10

Talking Points

1. A basic theme of the film is that noble *birth* is less important than noble *behavior*, and that William's knightly character is what makes him heroic. List the things he does that are truly virtuous. Point out that lying about his heritage and sleeping with Jocelyn were *not* noble, yet the latter is almost treated as a grand accomplishment rather than a moral failure. Discuss these things in light of 1 Corinthians 6:18-20, Hebrews 13:4, 1 Thessalonians 4:3-5, and Isaiah 5:20.

2. Once exposed as a fraud, William chooses to stay and face the music. Ask teens how they feel about his decision. Was it the right thing to do? Would they have done the same or heeded Will's friends' advice? For that matter, would they have committed the deception in the first place? Why or why not?

3. Explore the spiritual parallels between the prince's pardon of William and Jesus Christ's rescue of sinners saved by grace. Use verses such as Isaiah 55:6-7, 2 Corinthians 5:16-19, Romans 5:6-11 & 6:23, 1 Peter 2:9-10, Revelation 12:10, and Matthew 28:18.

4. Examine how the friends all pitch in to help William write a love letter, fix his armor, and prepare him for the dance. How does such loyalty and selflessness—especially following William's arrest—reflect Proverbs 17:17 and John 15:13?

5. Adhemar equates William's display of mercy with weakness. Conversely, Jocelyn finds William all the more attractive for it. Read Matthew 5:7 and 9:9-13 for God's view of mercy.

6. Talk about the film's references to God, Jesus, the church, and the Bible. On a scale of 1-10, how reverent do you think they are? Why?

7. Teenagers will no doubt identify with the giddy awkwardness William feels upon meeting Jocelyn. Tell your teen about a time when you might have felt that way about someone. Invite him or her to do the same. Take a moment to make a distinction between love-at-first-sight infatuation and the kind of character-based love and commitment that endures.

8. When William talks of "changing his stars," what does he mean? Is life mapped out in the cosmos as some astrologers suggest, or do we have the freedom to chart our own destiny? Read Proverbs 3:5-6 and 1 Corinthians 2:10-16.

9. Ask teens if they think William's dad did the right thing by sending

him off to serve as a squire. On one hand, it was Will's ticket out and a chance to get closer to his dream. On the other hand, father and son missed important years in their relationship.

Follow-Up Activity

Christian teens can use their newfound perspective on the film's closing scenes to share the gospel with unsaved friends familiar with the movie. It's a non-confrontational witnessing tool. Ask your teen if there's someone he or she has been praying for who would benefit from such a discussion. For adolescents who see the value in it but lack the confidence to proceed, invite them to practice on you.

Just for Fun

Making movies can be a dangerous business. The DVD commentary by writer/director/producer Brian Helgeland shows the filmmaker minus a front tooth which was accidentally knocked out by star Heath Ledger when the pair were demonstrating a joust with broom handles.

—*Bob Smithouser*

Life Is Beautiful

Rated: PG-13
Themes: Lust for life, sacrificial love, romance in marriage, anti-Semitism, making the best of a bad situation, a father's legacy to his son, horrors of the Holocaust
Running Time: 1 hour, 56 minutes
Starring: Roberto Benigni as Guido Orefice; Nicoletta Braschi as Dora; Giorgio Cantarini as Joshua
Directed by: Roberto Benigni

 ## Cautions

A couple of mild sexual references. For example, before they are married, Guido tells Dora, "You can't imagine how much I feel like making love to you . . . not once, but over and over again." Scenes in the concentration camp are intense, but not extremely graphic (there's a pile of human remains somewhat obscured by fog). It is implied that children and the elderly are killed in gas chambers. A man is machine-gunned to death offscreen. This is a film best shared with older teens.

 ## Story Summary

The most common image of a movie hero is probably someone like James Bond—a Renaissance man who can handle any weapon, drive any vehicle (with little or no instruction), and outwit the most devious criminal mind the writer can dream up. Most teens, if asked to create a champion, wouldn't begin to imagine Guido Orefice, a balding, slender, Italian bookshop owner who loves life and views everything as a wonderful adventure. In most films, Guido would be the comic relief. But in *Life Is Beautiful* he is that and much, much more.

We first meet Guido as he and a friend are driving through the Arrezo countryside on their way to the city in 1939. Their brakes fail, sending the car careening off the road, through the woods, and eventually past a crowd of people who mistake them for a royal motorcade. It's just one of many charming, comical moments in the film's first hour. As Guido pursues his dream of opening a bookshop, he waits tables for his Uncle Eliseo.

Guido's fortunes include meeting a beautiful young woman named Dora when she literally falls into his arms. Their paths cross again in several unusual and humorous ways, and Guido is smitten by this woman he calls "principessa" ("my princess"). As they get acquainted, we are treated to some delightful slapstick in the spirit of Charlie Chaplin. To complicate matters, Dora is engaged to a stodgy bureaucrat, but Guido wins her heart and rescues her from a drab future. They marry, have a son named Joshua, and Guido fulfills his dream of owning a bookshop.

World War II forms the backdrop for the story, and at the start of the second half of this two-act drama, Germany occupies Italy. Jews are rounded up. Guido, Eliseo, and three-year-old Joshua are forced to board a train that will carry them to a concentration camp. Dora arrives home to find them gone and rushes to the station where she demands to be put on the train with her husband, even though she isn't a Jew. The remainder of the movie follows the family as they attempt to survive the horrors of the holocaust.

Eliseo and other elderly prisoners unable to work are taken to the gas chamber, and we learn that all children in the camp will soon suffer a similar fate. To save his son's life, Guido concocts a story that everyone is a participant in a huge game. The first person to earn 1,000 points wins the grand prize—a *real* tank. Other children disappear (Guido tells the boy they're in hiding), but Joshua manages to avoid the guards. All of Guido's instructions (how to hide, never complain, remain silent in the company of Germans, etc.) are designed to protect his son and are phrased as rules that will earn points toward the grand prize.

Though Dora and Guido can't be together in the prison camp, their deep love and devotion are palpable. Every thought and action are geared toward their ultimate reunion as a family. As the war nears its conclusion and the allies approach the camp, German guards frantically destroy evidence of their unspeakable deeds. Prisoners are hastily herded onto trucks. Guido hides his son and searches for Dora to warn her that getting on a truck would mean certain death.

Guido is finally caught, and to save his son he bravely marches to his own execution. Just a few hours later, the prisoners are free. An American tank drives into the compound and the joyful boy knows he has won! Joshua gets a ride on the tank before sharing a jubilant reunion with his mother. We hear the grown-up voice of Joshua say, "This is my story. This is the sacrifice my father made. This was his gift to me."

• • •

NOTE: Teens may bristle at the thought of a foreign film with wall-to-wall subtitles. This Best Foreign Language Film of 1998 is worth the effort. It is an exceptional combination of comedy and pathos that is available in English, but we recommend that you watch it in Italian. After a few minutes, you'll hardly notice that you're reading.

Before You Watch

Ask teens to talk about their heroes, be they actors, sports figures, musicians, or even a fictional character like Superman or James Bond. Ask why they are attracted to this person. Be prepared to share some of the heroes from your youth, why they were important to you, and how you feel about them today.

A day or two before watching the film, play a game together. Something like *Battleship* or *Operation* would be great. The key is to choose one that uses a very serious, even life-and-death premise and makes a game of it. Just have fun. After watching the movie, you may want to refer back to the experience.

Bible Bookmarks

Gen. 1:26-27, 2:7; 1 Tim. 4:4; Phil. 2:5-8; Jn. 10:10, 15:13;
Ps. 49:7-9; Job 8:20-22; 1 Pet. 1:6-9; Eph. 5:22-23

Talking Points

1. What is Guido's philosophy of life? Why do you think he views life so positively? Do you think this reflects how God wants us to perceive it? To help answer this question, read Genesis 1:26-27 and 2:7. Then read 1 Timothy 4:4 and John 10:10.

2. Early in the film, Eliseo gives Guido instructions about how to be a good waiter. He says, "Serving is a supreme art. God is the first servant. God serves men, but He's not a servant to men." What do you think he meant? How does Philippians 2:5-8 apply? Does Guido reflect that attitude? What does Guido's joyfully serving others tell you?

3. What do you think makes Guido attractive to Dora? What makes her attractive to him? Neither of these actors would be considered gorgeous by Hollywood's standards. How important is physical beauty in romantic relationships? Is physical attraction the key to Guido and Dora's marriage? What is?

4. Dora's and Guido's love never wanes. What do you think keeps it so strong? Read Ephesians 5:22-33. Do you see Dora as this type of wife? How? In what ways does Guido love her sacrificially?

5. One of the most powerful scenes is at the train station. Dora can either go home and try to rebuild her life or get on the train and follow her family to the concentration camp. What compels her to get on the train? Would you do the same thing? Why or why not?

6. Guido wants to protect his son. How does he do it? What other options did he have?

7. In John 15:13, Jesus says that there is no greater love a man can show than to lay down his life for his friend. How did you feel as you saw Guido march to his execution? Did his death save his son? Now read Psalm 49:7-9. What did Guido's death do for his son? What could his death *not* do?

8. The German doctor who loved riddles had a chance to help Guido. Did he? How did the movie make you feel about this man?

9. What legacy did Guido's love give Joshua? Read Job 8:20-22 and discuss how this story reflects that philosophy. Did Guido and his uncle escape suffering?

10. Should we find ourselves faced with trials, pain, or suffering, how can we gain comfort and perspective from the words of 1 Peter 1:6-9?

Follow-Up Activity

Families wishing to learn more about this period in world history can start online at *A Teacher's Guide to the Holocaust* (fcit.coedu.usf.edu/holocaust), which includes lesson plans and activities for students of various ages.

Two popular books offering personal accounts of anti-Semitism are *Anne Frank: The Diary of a Young Girl* and Corrie Ten Boom's spiritual journey in the face of Nazi persecution, *The Hiding Place*.

Just for Fun

Guido plays a record over the loudspeaker to let Joshua and Dora (played by Benigni's real-life wife, Braschi) know he's all right. But it's an unlikely selection. He chooses "The Barcarole" from Offenbach's *The Tales of Hoffman*. However, since Offenbach was Jewish, it's doubtful his music would have been on the playlist at a Nazi concentration camp. Oops!

—*Al Janssen*

Little Women

Rated: PG
Themes: Delighting in one's family, generosity, modesty, forgiveness, true love, moral courage, gender equality
Running Time: 1 hour, 55 minutes
Starring: Winona Ryder as Jo; Kirsten Dunst and Samantha Mathis as Amy; Claire Danes as Beth; Trini Alvarado as Meg; Susan Sarandon as Marmee; Christian Bale as Laurie; Gabriel Byrne as Friedrich Bhaer
Directed by: Gillian Armstrong

Cautions

Some social drinking. A few intense moments (Amy falls through the ice, Beth succumbs to a serious illness, etc.) but nothing objectionable.

Story Summary

In the early 1860s, as the Civil War rages on, lamp oil is scarce and the ladies of the March family are trying to make the best of things in Concord, Mass., while father serves his country. The eldest daughter, Meg, is proper and kind. Jo, the impulsive tomboy, has a wild streak and loves to write creative stories. Beth is tender and quiet. It seems her only ambition involves basking in the sweetness of family time. Amy comes across as winsome, romantic, and perhaps a bit spoiled as the youngest in the clan. Their mother, Marmee, is a wise matriarch and mid-19th-century feminist who teaches her girls to live beyond what society has allotted for them. They all share a strong home filled with love, laughter, and a generous spirit.

As young girls, Meg, Beth, Jo, and Amy hold great expectations for their lives. They dream big dreams and fantasize about the perfect husband. Days are spent curling one another's hair, acting out Jo's plays in the attic, and reading letters from their father. Then they make a new friend when their rigid neighbor takes in his grandson, Laurie. The young man is fresh off the boat from Europe where he was educated in order to attend college stateside and learn his grandfather's banking business. Much of Laurie's joy comes from hanging out with the March family. He's the brother they never had.

The story, which focuses mostly on Jo, spans a five-year period during which various experiences draw the sisters closer and strengthen their love for each other. Some moments are fun. Some involve sacrifice. Others end in rejoicing, still others in tragedy. As each girl matures, she chooses the type of woman she will be, the man she will marry, and the priorities that will guide her destiny. For Jo, that includes earning respect as a writer.

Like many adolescents, Jo is torn between love of family and a clawing desire to experience the world ("I love our home but I'm just so fitful that I can't stand being here . . . I just know I'll never fit in anywhere"). It's universal teen angst, Victorian style. With Marmee's help, Jo moves to New York City where she writes, teaches, and works at a boarding house. That's where she meets Friedrich Bhaer, a middle-aged German philosophy professor who becomes her mentor, friend, and eventually her fiancée. He recognizes her talent and challenges her to advance beyond lurid melodramas and write from somewhere deeper.

Informed that Beth's health is failing, Jo returns home to be with her sister. They talk about their childhood and the paths everyone has chosen. By now Meg is married and pregnant with twins. Amy has gone to Europe with Aunt March. The only one who hasn't "moved on" is Beth, who confesses to Jo, "I love being home. I just don't like being left behind." After Beth passes from this life to the next, Jo discovers a trunk full of things she treasured— mementos from their youth. Inspired by Beth's life and Friedrich's words, Jo puts her heart and soul into writing a very personal novel which is later published, offering the world a glimpse at the most important thing in her life . . . her family.

Before You Watch

If your teen enjoys playacting, find a book of one-act plays or youth-group skits and read through a couple as a family in the days prior to your Movie Night. Really get into the characters and have fun. Who knows, it may turn into a fun activity that yields memories for your family like the ones shared by the March sisters.

Bible Bookmarks

Eph. 4:26; 1 Pet. 3:3-4; Ps. 32:8; Prov. 3:5-6, 16:9, 28:2-5; Col. 3:12-14; 2 Cor. 9:6-11

Talking Points

1. The sisters elect to give their Christmas breakfast to a needy family and do so with a cheerful attitude. Without complaining, Jo sells her hair to pay for Marmee's travel expenses. Can you remember any instances of sacrificial giving in your family? Read 2 Corinthians 9:6-11 for a promise from God on the subject of sacrificial generosity.

2. The March parents have different means of "standing up to the lions of injustice," one with the pen (Marmee's angry letter to Amy's teacher), the other with the sword (father's military service). Ask teens which they identify with more closely, and if they think one method is preferable to the other.

3. After Amy burns Jo's manuscript, Marmee quotes Ephesians 4:26 to try to keep the peace. Read that verse aloud and talk about the wisdom in it. What consequences might befall us if we *don't* follow that command?

4. Meg gives in to peer pressure and compromises her propriety by letting the girls make her up for the party. When her uncharacteristically immodest, flirtatious behavior gets challenged by Laurie, Meg states, "I was only playing a part." Still, she realizes he's right and that it reflects poorly on her. In 2001, pop idol Britney Spears defended her sexual stage

antics by saying much the same thing—without any apologies. Is "playing a part" an excuse to act irresponsibly? Talk about the lesson Meg learned.

5. Jo and her family knew from a young age that she had a gift and a passion for writing. Ask teens to identify their own gifts. What are their passions? The two can combine to help us forge more realistic, fulfilling pursuits in life. Read Proverbs 16:9 and discuss practical steps you can take together to nurture your teen's gifts and passions.

6. The March sisters discuss the relative importance of money when choosing a mate. How important is wealth to a healthy marriage? Why? Invite teens to share the qualities they're looking for in their future spouse.

7. Which sister was your favorite and why? Which was your *least* favorite and why? What about the men they chose as husbands?

8. Do you think Jo did the right thing by turning down Laurie's proposal and later marrying a man twice her age? Why or why not? Do you think Laurie truly loved Amy, or was he more enamored with being part of the March family? What made you think that?

9. How do you think Christian faith (demonstrated in prayer, Bible reading, and the singing of spiritual songs) made the March family stronger? What other virtues seemed to knit them together? Ask, "Why are they important for our family as well?" Discuss the relevance of Colossians 3:12-14.

10. Examine the way the sisters entertained themselves and one another with books, drama, and music. Had there been television, stereo headphones, and video games back then, would the girls have grown as close? Why or why not? How can you and your children "make your own fun" in a more active, creative way?

11. Discuss the following quotes. What did they mean in the context of the story? How do they apply to your life?

• Amy's statement, "We'll all grow up someday. We might as well know what we want." (Psalm 32:8, Proverbs 3:5-6)

• Their mother's regret, "I wish I could give my girls a more just world." (Proverbs 28:2-5)

• Marmee's philosophy, "If you feel your value lies in being merely decorative, I fear that someday you will believe that's all you really are. Time erodes all such beauty, but what it cannot diminish is the wonderful workings of your mind—your humor, your kindness, your moral courage." (1 Peter 3:3-4)

Follow-Up Activity

Create a "family newspaper" to send out with your holiday greeting cards. Let each family member choose a "story" to cover from the past year. If someone in the group isn't fond of writing, invite that person to design the page. You can start working on it at any time and watch it evolve as the year goes on.

Is there a needy family you can adopt as the Marches adopted the Hummels? Can you think of creative ways to help and encourage them? Consider leaving an anonymous gift of add-water cookie mix, coupons for a local movie theater, fast-food gift certificates, etc. Pray about who to choose and what to do. God may even offer you a chance to share Jesus or invite them to church.

Just for Fun

Since Louisa May Alcott's classic novel was first published in 1868, *Little Women* has been translated into 30 languages, proving that universal themes transcend cultural boundaries.

—Lissa Johnson

The Mission

Rated: PG
Themes: Conversion, missionary outreach, defending the weak, martyrdom, pacifism vs. self-defense
Running Time: 2 hours, 5 minutes
Starring: Jeremy Irons as Father Gabriel; Robert DeNiro as Captain Rodrigo Mendoza; Liam Neeson as Fielding; Aidan Quinn as Felipe; Ray McAnally as Cardinal Altamirano
Directed by: Roland Joffé

Cautions

The opening scene shows a crucified priest being swept over a massive waterfall. There are several passing glimpses of female Indians' breasts, and a parting scene shows preadolescent natives completely naked (all with a *National Geographic* feel). There are two mild profanities. Haunting violence in the final 20 minutes features invading soldiers trying to remove the Indians from the mission. Children are shot, fighting men on both sides get knifed, shot, hit with arrows, run through with swords, and swept over the falls.

Story Summary

Based on actual events, this film takes place in 1750 around the borders of Argentina, Paraguay, and Brazil. A cardinal, dictating a letter to the pope, narrates the story which begins with a powerful image: A missionary priest, tied to a cross, is sent down the river and over a raging waterfall by the Indians he was trying to reach.

The death of this priest doesn't deter the Jesuits. Father Gabriel makes the difficult journey into the jungle and begins to reach out to the

Indians. At the same time, the natives are terrorized by a slave trader, Captain Rodrigo Mendoza. Upon returning from one of his forays, Mendoza learns that his brother loves the same woman he does. In a fit of anger Mendoza kills his brother. When he realizes what he has done, Mendoza seeks sanctuary in the church and languishes in a cell.

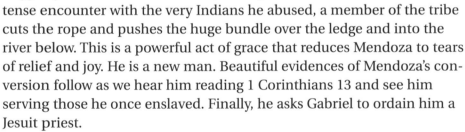

Six months later, Gabriel is asked to talk to Mendoza. But the mercenary is morose, believing there's no redemption for him. Gabriel comes up with a unique therapy. For days, Mendoza totes a huge net through the jungle filled with armor and weapons representing his past and his sins. He doggedly carries the burden until, during a tense encounter with the very Indians he abused, a member of the tribe cuts the rope and pushes the huge bundle over the ledge and into the river below. This is a powerful act of grace that reduces Mendoza to tears of relief and joy. He is a new man. Beautiful evidences of Mendoza's conversion follow as we hear him reading 1 Corinthians 13 and see him serving those he once enslaved. Finally, he asks Gabriel to ordain him a Jesuit priest.

Meanwhile, a three-way political conflict involves Spain, Portugal, and the church. Currently the missionary efforts are protected by Spain. But a treaty has given this land over to Portugal, which intends to use the Indians as slave labor on their plantations. The cardinal must decide whether or not to protect the missions, which are the Indians' only hope. Inevitably, political and business interests supercede ministry to the natives. The Jesuits are ordered to abandon their work and the people they've invested in. Neither Gabriel nor Mendoza is willing to leave, but troops are on their way to forcibly evict the Indians. Gabriel turns to prayer. Mendoza wants to fight.

Mendoza: They want to live, Father. They say that God has left them, deserted them. Has He?

Gabriel: You should never have become a priest.

Mendoza: But I am a priest and they need me.

88

Gabriel: Then help them *as* a priest. If you die with blood on your hands, Rodrigo, you betray everything we've done. You promised your life to God, and God is *love!*

The film's final 20 minutes are compelling, yet disturbing. Mendoza prepares for battle, rallying some of the Jesuit brothers and men from the tribe. Gabriel gathers women and children into the church to pray. It is a hopeless situation. The Indians, with primitive weapons, cannot thwart the European soldiers. There is no miraculous rescue. The mission is overrun. And the political powers of the time have won . . . or have they?

Before You Watch

Consider watching this film in early November. The first Sunday of the month is the International Day of Prayer for the persecuted church around the world. During dinner, ask teens for their impressions of missions. What does it take to be a missionary? What dangers exist? If you know some missionaries, tell a story about their work.

Bible Bookmarks

Ps. 11; Matt. 5:10, 16:24-26, 28:18-20; 1 Cor. 13; Acts 1:8; Heb. 11:36-40; Rev. 2:10, 6:9-11

Talking Points

The following are difficult questions. Theologians have debated why God allows bad things to happen to good people. You may not come up with nice, neat answers. Still, the questions are worth asking so you and your teen can begin formulating answers in the safety of your home.

1. Discuss the brief exchange reprinted in the story summary. With which character did you most identify, Father Gabriel (who prefers peaceful resistance and leading people in prayer) or Rodrigo Mendoza (who chooses to defend the village and resist the soldiers)? Why? Talk about the *opposite* choice and any merits or weaknesses of it.

2. How do you respond to David's question in Psalm 11:3? What can the righteous do in a situation like the one faced by this mission? Note

how David's perspective changes in verse 4. Do his words affect how you view the events portrayed in the film? If so, how?

3. The cardinal knew the expectations of his superiors. What could he have done differently? Read Matthew 16:24-26. Do Jesus' words provide any insight into the cardinal's situation?

4. Talk about Mendoza's conversion. Was anything missing you wish had been included? What changes did you see in his life? What convinced you it was genuine?

5. The following passage from John Bunyan's book *Pilgrim's Progress* depicts the conversion of its main character, named Christian. Read it aloud and then discuss the similarity of this scene with the dramatic conversion of Mendoza:

"Now I saw in my dream, that the highway up which CHRISTIAN was to go was fenced on either side with a wall; and that wall was called 'Salvation.' Up this way, therefore, did burdened CHRISTIAN run; but not without great difficulty, because of the load on his back.

"He ran thus till he came at a place somewhat ascending; and upon that place stood a Cross, and a little below, in the bottom, a sepulchre. So I saw in my dream, that just as CHRISTIAN came up with the cross, his burden loosed from off his shoulders, and fell from off his back, and began to tumble; and so continued to do till it came to the mouth of the sepulchre, where it fell in, and I saw it no more.

"Then was CHRISTIAN glad . . ."

6. After his transformation, Mendoza reads 1 Corinthians 13 as we see him interacting with the Indians. Read it together and discuss how Mendoza lived out this "love chapter."

7. How did you feel about the ending? Did you have a sense of hopelessness? Why or why not? Was the sacrifice made by the priests and Indians worth the cost? Why? Why do you think God allowed this tragedy to occur? Can you think of any good that might have come of it?

8. There are people suffering injustice today. In Sudan, Christian tribes are being forced off the land and into slavery. In Colombia, Christians are caught between drug lords and government troops. In many Muslim countries, it is illegal for Christians to meet together or talk to Muslims about their faith. Jesus said in Matthew 5:10, "Blessed are those who are persecuted because of righteousness, for theirs is the kingdom of heaven." How do you think this verse applies to the Indians and missionaries in this film? How does it apply to persecuted Christians today?

9. The Bible openly talks about the possibility that we might die for our Lord. Each year more than 150,000 people around the world become martyrs, killed because of their Christian faith. Read Revelation 2:10, 6:9-11, and Hebrews 11:36-40. Do you think Gabriel, Mendoza, and the Indians in their mission could be classified as martyrs? Can you conceive of any situation where you might be challenged to die for your faith? How do you think you'd respond?

Follow-Up Activity

Read Matthew 28:18-20 and Acts 1:8, key passages addressing Christian missionary activity. If you support a missionary, learn more about what he or she does. Or ask about a missionary your church supports. If your teen shows interest in foreign missions, discuss the possibility of a short-term tour of duty. Better yet, perhaps you can go on a missions trip together.

For more information about persecuted brothers and sisters abroad, you can contact Open Doors at P.O. Box 27001, Santa Ana, CA 92799 or visit their Web site at: www.opendoorsusa.org.

Just for Fun

Ironically, Robert DeNiro, known for playing tough guys on-screen, caught the acting bug at age 10 when he portrayed the Cowardly Lion in a local stage production of *The Wizard of Oz.*

—Al Janssen

Mr. Holland's Opus

Rated: PG
Themes: Making one's life count, personal goals vs. responsibility, marital fidelity, coping with a child's disabilities
Running Time: 2 hours, 23 minutes
Starring: Richard Dreyfuss as Glenn Holland; Glenne Headley as Iris; Jay Thomas as Bill; Olympia Dukakis as Principal Jacobs; William H. Macy as Vice Principal Wolters; Alicia Witt as Gertrude; Jean Louisa Kelly as Rowena
Directed by: Stephen Herek

Cautions

The dialogue includes ten profanities (mild except for one b—s——, a g—d——, and two uses of a—h——).

Story Summary

The late John Lennon penned the lyric, "Life is what happens to you when you're busy making other plans." Few films have illustrated that truth with more warmth and wit than *Mr. Holland's Opus*. It opens in the mid-1960s with one man's dream. More than anything, 30-year-old Glenn Holland wants to write a symphony. But while he possesses the talent, *time* comes at a premium. A starving composer, Holland needs full-time employment to support himself and his wife, Iris. He lands what he thinks is a "temporary gig" as a high school music teacher ("Like most people, I only got my teaching certificate so I'd have something to fall back on"). It's an awkward transition. As he spends untold hours preparing lessons, trying to connect with students, and teaching driver's ed for extra summer cash, his unfinished symphony collects dust.

Several years go by. Holland is still in the classroom, encouraging teens to reach for the stars. He has learned to use rock 'n' roll to connect with students. He's even in charge of the marching band. However, just as he seems to be hitting stride as an educator, Holland's infant son, Cole, is discovered to be almost entirely deaf. Unable to draw the child into his musical world, he struggles to find common ground and chooses to immerse himself in work while Iris focuses on learning how to communicate with Cole. The notion of "spare time" is a myth. And Holland's symphony—along with his neglected family—waits patiently in the wings.

A montage of '60s and '70s newsreel footage marks the passage of time. Graduating classes come and go. Holland's frustration mounts as the daily grind continues to distract him from zealously pursuing his musical masterpiece. While producing the senior musical—a Gershwin revue—he develops an attraction to the pretty young lead, but chooses to resist her advances. Immediately afterward, his strained relationship with Cole reaches a turning point with the death of John Lennon. Cole's dad assumes that he can't understand the loss or appreciate the former Beatle's cultural significance simply because he's deaf. An outraged Cole passionately explains that he loves music even though he can't hear it. The bond between father and son improves. In fact, Holland even produces a live concert sensitive to the needs of the deaf, during which he sings a tender ballad to his son.

Years pass. The board of education decides to cut the school's music program due to a lack of funds. Now 60 years old, Holland is forced to retire. He returns to the school with his family to pack up his belongings and, before leaving the building for the last time, he hears a commotion in the auditorium only to discover a surprise farewell tribute in his honor. Two generations of students have gathered to express their appreciation and perform, for the first time, the very arrangement Holland has been writing since he started teaching. As the movie ends, a tearful Mr. Holland conducts his opus.

Glenn Holland comes to realize

that the constant interruptions to his lifelong ambition were *themselves* the stuff dreams are made of: Bonding with his only son. Inspiring young people to greatness and a love of music. During Holland's 30-year journey, many lives are miraculously transformed—none more dramatically than his own. But beyond tugging heartstrings, this Oscar-nominated film is also quite humorous in places. During a driver's ed lesson, Holland's panicked pupil jumps a curb and parks in a flower bed. Instead of flying off the handle, the slightly shaken teacher calmly asks, "Okay, what have we learned from this?" Adults might ask the same question of their teenagers after viewing this touching film together.

Before You Watch

What's your teen's passionate dream (playing an instrument, writing a novel, healing the sick, painting a mural, owning a business, etc.)? Is the goal short-term or long-term? Is there a specific plan for making it happen? See if the daily responsibilities at home, school, or work are getting in the way of fulfilling that dream, and what you might do to free up your teen to pursue it more aggressively.

Bible Bookmarks

Gal. 6:9; Jas. 1:13-18, 3:3-12; Matt. 19:4-6; Heb. 13:4

Talking Points

1. Ask teens, "As you observed the film's portrayal of high school life in the 1960s, what did you find similar to or different from your present-day experience?" and "With which student in the movie did you most identify? Why?"

2. Principal Jacobs tells Holland that his duties include giving young minds a "compass" so that their knowledge doesn't go to waste. What does she mean? Do you have any teachers who do that well? How have they been an encouragement to you?

3. Mr. Holland asks Gertrude, "When you look in the mirror, what do you like best about yourself? Why?" Ask your teen the same question. The answer may surprise you. Be prepared to share several things *you* find attractive about your teen (physical features are fine, but virtuous character traits are even better).

4. Wolters and Holland get into an argument about the merits of using rock 'n' roll in music class. Try to look at the situation from both men's perspectives. In what ways does each have a valid point? Urge teens to put themselves in the position of the mediator, Principal Jacobs. Did she handle the conflict appropriately? Why or why not?

5. In desperation, Iris cries, *"I can't talk to my son.* I don't know what he wants or what he thinks or what he feels. I can't tell him that I love him. I can't tell him who I am. I want to talk to my son. I don't care what it costs." Put yourself in her place. How must it feel to be a mother in that situation? As parent and teen, do you sometimes take your ability to communicate for granted? Have you ever *abused* that gift (James 3:3-12)? How can the Hollands' frustration impart a deeper appreciation of the ability to share intimately in your home?

6. Discuss the following quotes. What did they mean in the context of the story? What do they mean to you?

• "The most important teacher your child will ever have is you."

• "Play the sunset."

• "We are your symphony, Mr. Holland. We are the melodies and the notes of your opus and we are the music of your life."

7. Examine Holland's attraction to Rowena. What does God's Word say about infidelity in Matthew 19:4-6, Hebrews 13:4, and James 1:13-18? How did professional frustrations and domestic stress help to create an environment where temptation could enter in? What could Holland have done differently to keep this near-fling from going as far as it did? Even though he ultimately made the right choice, how do you think this affected his marriage?

8. Holland gives a concert during which he uses lights to interpret rhythm to the deaf members of his audience. Why was this such a significant step for him? If you were a *visual* artist, how would you describe your work to a person who was born blind?

9. How are Holland's years of faithfulness (to the educational community and to his family) rewarded in the film's closing scene? What might have happened had he walked away from it all and accompanied Rowena during a season of weakness in his life? What can we learn from his example? Read Galatians 6:9 for a biblical perspective.

 **Follow-Up Activity**

Dust off your high school yearbook and page through it

with your teen. Look at the hairstyles, fashions, and so on and compare these snapshots to a time period introduced in the film. Invite your teens to ask about the people and places pictured there.

Mr. Holland's first real breakthrough with his students came when he asked them what kind of music they liked and connected *his* theory to *their* world. We can do the same with our own children. With movies. With sports. With whatever excites them. Look for ways to enter your teen's world this week. Once you start having *fun* together, teachable moments will follow.

Just for Fun

On the way to the hospital, the driver-training car loses a hubcap while taking a corner at high speed. Count the hubcaps as it pulls into the parking lot. Oops!

—Shana Murph

October Sky

Rated: PG
Running Time: 1 hour, 48 minutes
Themes: Following an "impossible" dream, father/son conflict, quest for parental approval, perseverance, sibling rivalry, family unity in tough times, the power of a supportive mentor/community
Starring: Jake Gyllenhaal as Homer Hickam; Chris Cooper as John Hickam; Laura Dern as Miss Frieda Riley; Natalie Canerday as Elsie Hickam; with Chris Owen, Chad Lindberg, and William Lee Scott
Directed by: Joe Johnston

Cautions

Mild violence. Profanities are common, but the majority are relatively tame (SOB, h——, d—n). Homer's buddy mocks virginity and coaches him on stealthily touching a girl's breast. The boys steal some materials to build their launch site and rockets. They also appear tipsy after visiting a moonshiner to get pure alcohol to use as rocket fuel.

Story Summary

This inspirational biography, infused with humor and classic rock tunes, is set in the coal-mining town of Coalwood, West Virginia, in October 1957, just after the Soviets put the first satellite, Sputnik, into earth's orbit. Mining is a way of life in Coalwood. Most local residents work for "the company," which owns employees' homes and nearly every building in town—including the church. Boys growing up there seem destined to inherit a place in the dark, dangerous mine, except perhaps the lucky few who manage to attend college on football scholarships.

In one 17-year-old, however, the sight of Sputnik streaking across the night sky sparks a dream. Homer Hickam dares to hope that one day he could become a NASA scientist. But unlike his athletic brother, Jim, Homer's shot at college seems remote. Still, his fascination with rockets, coupled with the encouragement of his idealistic teacher Miss Riley, leads him to convince his buddies O'Dell and Roy Lee—as well as Quentin, the school geek—to begin building rockets in hopes of winning the national science fair in Indianapolis. More than just a gold medal, the victors receive academic scholarships.

Homer's father, John, is the mine foreman, an alternately heroic and narrow-mindedly combustible personality who disapproves of Homer's pursuits. In John's view, his son's dream is an absurd affront to the noble call of mining. Homer needs to grow up, forget about rocketry (except as a hobby), and proudly follow him underground. This clash of dreams and expectations is the story's central conflict.

Through trial and error, always learning from mistakes, Homer and his friends build and launch a series of rockets from a barren site eight miles outside of town. Early attempts result in spectacular, explosive failures. Gradually though, with help from a couple of mining-company welders, their designs and fuels improve. Unfortunately, just when they achieve their first big success, one of their stray rockets gets blamed for starting a forest fire. The Rocket Boys get shut down. Homer's dream seems dead.

Things go from bad to worse when his dad is seriously hurt after a shaft collapses. In a selfless act of responsibility to his family, Homer drops out of school to grab a pickaxe and miner's helmet so that Jim can go on to college. Despite an enduring hatred for the mine, Homer is willing to choke on coal dust until Dad gets back on his feet.

The story takes another turn when Homer visits Miss Riley, who he learns has Hodgkin's disease. She encourages him, "Sometimes you really can't listen to what anybody else says. You've just gotta listen inside." He's inspired. Homer returns to his study of rocketry and proves that their rocket could *not* have started the forest fire. A local hero once again, he abandons the mine, re-enrolls in school, and enters the county science fair.

A fully recovered John Hickam isn't pleased. But his son insists, "The coal mine is *your* life. It's not mine. I'm never going down there again. I want to go into space." The boys go on to win the county science fair and elect Homer to represent the team in Indianapolis. As he prepares to leave, the local miners go on strike. Then, on the eve of the judging at the national science fair, a key part of the boys' display is stolen. To get it replaced in time, Elsie Hickam urges her husband to swallow his pride and settle the strike so that the machinists can help. John comes through, as do his men.

With all of Coalwood pulling for them, the Rocket Boys win first prize. Each receives a college scholarship. At the launch of their last rocket, named in honor of the now bedridden Miss Riley, Homer's dad makes a surprise appearance. Showing maturity and forgiveness, Homer invites him to push the button, and the two are reconciled. As this charming true story ends, viewers get to see grainy home video of the actual people portrayed onscreen, as well as information about what they went on to accomplish in life.

Before You Watch

Tour a workplace with your teen that's loud, hot, dirty, dark, or even a little dangerous (compared to, say, a desk job). Then go out for pizza and ask, "Suppose all the adults in our family, going back generations, had worked in a place like that, not out of *choice*, but because it was the only employer in town and it was all they knew. Some had died in work-related accidents, others from diseases they'd picked up there. Suppose everyone expected *you* to work there long-term too, and you really didn't have any other options. How would you feel about that? Why? Would you be content to work there? If not, how might you try to chart another course?"

Bible Bookmarks
Eph. 4:29, 6:1-4; 2 Cor. 5:16-21; Matt. 9:9-13

Talking Points

1. Ephesians 6:1-4 tells children to honor their parents. How well did Homer do that? Was he right or wrong to reach for the stars? Why? That passage also instructs fathers to resist "exasperating" their children. How well did John Hickam do at that? How so?

2. Do you think Homer and his dad could have found reconciliation sooner? What would it have taken? Read about our call to a "ministry of reconciliation" in 2 Corinthians 5:16-21. How does that relate to the family? Ask "What can we learn from Homer and John Hickam's experience that will help us to better handle our next family conflict?"

3. Late in the film, as Homer tries to make peace with his dad, he says, "I come to believe that I got it in me to be somebody in this world. And it's not because I'm so different from you, either. It's because I'm the same. I can be just as hardheaded and just as tough." Ask teens, "In what ways are we alike? How is that good? How is that not so good? Why?"

4. What does this story tell you about human nature? The human spirit? The ability of a person to work hard, take risks, and pursue a goal in the face of big obstacles?

5. Which character in the movie do you most admire? Why?

6. Do you have an encourager like Miss Riley in your life? If so, who is it? If not, where might you find one that models Ephesians 4:29? Ask, "How can we better support each other in the pursuit of our dreams?"

7. Our society often belittles small-town morality as being outdated and irrelevant. How would you describe the worldview of the people who made this film? What things do they believe to be true and important about life?

8. When Miss Riley plays the radio for her class, the announcer divides time by stating, "It's the radio signal transmitted by the Soviet Sputnik. Listen now for the sound that forevermore separates the old from the new." The events of September 11, 2001 similarly separated the old from the new. Compare the impact both had on high school students.

9. The film revisits a time when creativity, a thirst for knowledge, and pure exploration filled after-school hours. Has that been lost in this age of MTV, DVD, and lifelike video games, or has it simply taken other forms? Explain.

10. Early on, Homer risks social suicide by sitting with Quentin. Although he does it for selfish reasons at first, the boys develop a solid

bond. Jesus wasn't above sitting with outcasts (Matthew 9:9-13). Ask, "Do you know of an outcast at school who you could reach out to?" It might be awkward at first, but it could lead to a great friendship.

Follow-Up Activity

October Sky is based on Homer Hickam's autobiographical book, *Rocket Boys*. If your teen enjoys reading, encourage him or her to ask for it at your local library.

Just for Fun

Here's a fun piece of trivia: If your family is big into word puzzles, you may have already noticed that scrambling the letters in *Rocket Boys* will yield . . . *October Sky*.

—*Larry Weeden*

The Princess Bride

Rated: PG
Themes: Heroism, revenge, pride, cowardice, true love, faithfulness, teamwork
Running Time: 1 hour, 38 minutes
Starring: Cary Elwes as Westley; Robin Wright as Buttercup; Mandy Patinkin as Inigo Montoya; Chris Sarandon as Prince Humperdinck; Christopher Guest as Count Rugen; Wallace Shawn as Vizzini; André the Giant as Fezzik; Billy Crystal as Miracle Max; Fred Savage as The Grandson; Peter Falk as Grandpa
Directed by: Rob Reiner

Cautions

While not unduly graphic, violence includes swordplay, stabbings, malicious torture, and a life-and-death struggle with a rodent of unusual size. Inigo gets drunk. The grandson uses Jesus' name as an exclamation (following Inigo and Fezzik's discovery of Westley in the Pit of Despair, just hit the mute button after the grandson says, "You mean he wins?"). The only other language involves a single use of "my god" and "son of a b——."

Story Summary

The Princess Bride is a fun, generally wholesome comedy/adventure. It follows the conventions of a classic fairy tale, but is quite unconventional. Its lighthearted humor and memorable one-liners have made it a favorite among youth groups and Christian college students who enjoy reciting its clever dialogue.

A young boy lies sick in bed. Not deathly ill, mind you, just sick enough to stay home from school, eat junk food, and play video games. He groans when his crusty, cheek-pinching grandfather comes to spend the day with him. He rolls his eyes all the more when Grandpa flips off the video game and opens a novel ("When I was your age, television was called books"). But it doesn't take long for the unfolding story to capture the boy's imagination. *The Princess Bride* brings a fairy tale to life in all its wistful glory. Sword fights. Tests of skill. Revenge. Giants. Monsters. Chases. Escapes. True love.

In the kingdom of Florin, beautiful Buttercup falls in love with a lowly farm boy named Westley. In order to earn enough money to be worthy of her hand, Westley seeks his fortune across the sea. As he leaves, he promises to return for her. Buttercup's heart is broken when she learns that her love's ship has been attacked by the Dread Pirate Roberts, a notorious scoundrel who takes no prisoners.

Soon afterward, Florin's arrogant Prince Humperdinck chooses the forlorn Buttercup as his showpiece bride. He announces their engagement to gain the approval of the common people, then arranges to have her killed in an attempt to frame his archenemy, the King of Gilder, giving Humperdink just cause to start a war. To do his dirty work, Humperdinck hires a ragamuffin band of thieves (Vizzini, a scheming Sicilian who's not as smart as he thinks he is; Fezzik, a slow giant with a pure heart; and Inigo, a Spaniard dedicated to avenging his father's murder). They kidnap Buttercup, but their plans get upended when a mysterious stranger catches up to them.

The stranger beats each man at his particular strength, all the while treating each with professional respect, and rescues the princess. Buttercup, believing her rescuer is the Dread Pirate Roberts, pushes him down a steep hill, only to find out that the stranger is actually her true love, Westley. She throws herself down the hill after him, then the reunited couple is pursued by Humperdinck, escaping into the perilous Fire Swamp only to be captured on the other side. Westley is sent to be tortured as his royal nemesis deceives and prepares to wed Buttercup. Poor Westley gets strapped to a table and has most of the life sucked out of him before Fezzik and Inigo come to his aid and take him to the hovel of Miracle Max, where the gnarled apothecary produces a potent pick-me-up. From there, the trio races (as fast as can be expected since they're forced to carry a still-limp Westley) to free Buttercup before the nuptials are complete. In the process, Inigo finds his father's murderer and squares off against him, getting his revenge (avoid the SOB line by pressing the mute button after Inigo miraculously revives and stabs his enemy). After a series of events, by turns noble, daring, and humorous, the princess is saved and the group is reunited. And Westley and his love live happily ever after.

Before You Watch

Around the dinner table have everyone share a positive memory of a sick day spent at home.

Talk about favorite childhood fairytales. What do many of these stories have in common? In other words, what makes a compelling story? (See Appendix II for common story structure elements.)

Bible Bookmarks

Matt. 20:28; Lk. 22:26; Gal. 5:13-14; Prov. 8:13, 11:2, 16:18; Acts 17:31; Rom. 12:4-8, 19; 1 Cor. 12:13-27; Jn. 1:10-12; Heb. 10:30-31, Jdg. 4

Talking Points

1. What is Westley's attitude toward Buttercup at the beginning of the story? How does his consistent service change her contempt for him into sincere affection? Read Matthew 20:28, Luke 22:26, and Galatians 5:13-14. What example did Jesus set for us in the area of service? Ask these questions: "How do we serve each other in our family?" "Do we ever take each other for granted?" "What can we do to serve each other better?" Aim for specifics.

2. Early in the story, Grandpa reads, "That day, [Buttercup] was amazed to discover that when [Westley] was saying 'As you wish,' what he meant was, 'I love you.'" Sometimes parents say "I love you" to their

children in ways that are difficult for teens to understand (holding them to a curfew, denying them certain things, building character in ways the teen finds unpleasant, etc.). Talk about this. Help your teen to start hearing "I love you" in the midst of caring, reasonable rules and discipline.

3. What in Westley's attitude makes him a hero? What does he have in common with heroes from other favorite stories, including Bible stories? For teen girls, recall scriptural conquests of Deborah or Esther (see Judges 4 and the book of Esther).

4. Was it fair for Westley to toy with Buttercup's emotions before their spill down the hill? Why or why not?

5. What does Humperdinck do that makes him a coward? What other flaws make him unworthy of our rooting interest?

6. Read Proverbs 8:13, 11:2, and 16:18. How does Humperdinck's arrogance set him up for defeat?

7. Inigo wants to avenge his father's death, and it seems he is satisfied once he kills Count Rugen. See what the Bible has to say about vengeance and justice in Romans 12:19, Acts 17:31, and Hebrews 10:30-31. How can movies manipulate us into rooting for someone like Inigo even when we know his quest is morally misguided?

8. Which character in the movie do you most admire? Why? How would you describe the worldview of the people who crafted this fairy tale, specifically the things they believe to be true and important about life?

9. Westley, Inigo, and Fezzik use different strengths (brains, skill, and brawn) to defeat Humperdinck. And they all admit that they couldn't have done it alone. What does the Bible say about using our different gifts for God? Read Romans 12:4-8 and 1 Corinthians 12:13-27.

10. In Buttercup's dream, the old peasant woman accuses her of turning her back on Westley's love: "True love saved her in the Fire Swamp and she treated it like garbage." Read John 1:10-12. How do humans treat Christ's sacrifice with contempt?

Follow-Up Activity

Inigo and Fezzik may start out as mercenaries, but at least they show honorable tendencies. For instance, Inigo helps Westley up the cliff and allows him to catch his breath before their duel. Fezzik complains that the way Vizzini wants Westley eliminated is "not very sportsmanlike." Teens raised in an age of terrorism and blast-every-thing-that-moves video games have little concept of "just war" and treating enemies with dignity. It may come as a surprise, even to parents, that the originator of "Just War Theory" was St. Thomas Aquinas, a devout Christian and great thinker of the early church. The funny fight scenes from this film may provide an opportunity to talk about biblical principles for fighting fair. For a more academic understanding of Just War Theory, refer to the Internet Encyclopedia of Philosophy at www.utm.edu/research/iep/j/justwar.htm, or pick up the *Summa Theologicae* for more about Aquinas's time-honored philosophy.

Just for Fun

Have you ever watched a movie and recognized a familiar voice, but had a hard time putting your finger on where you heard it before? Like a lot of viewers, you may get that sense when listening to Wallace Shawn, the actor who plays Vizzini. His voice is probably best known in connection with a computer-animated Disney character. Need a hint? A pal to Buzz and Woody, his moment of triumph in *Toy Story 2* finds him shouting, "I did it. I finally defeated Zurg!"

—*Lindy Beam*

Quiz Show

Rated: PG-13
Themes: Honesty, integrity, the slippery slope of compromise, unhealthy pride, family unity, anti-Semitism, the power of the media, quests for validation
Running Time: 2 hours, 13 minutes
Starring: Ralph Fiennes as Charles Van Doren; John Turturro as Herb Stempel; Rob Morrow as Dick Goodwin; David Paymer as Dan Enright; Paul Scofield as Mark Van Doren; Christopher MacDonald as Jack Barry; Hank Azaria as Albert Freedman
Directed by: Robert Redford

Cautions

Apart from frequent tobacco use, this rich character study presents just one hurdle: *language.* Five s-words, a use of the f-word, and 14 misuses of God's name are among the film's three dozen profanities/crude expressions. Therefore, we strongly recommend that families either use filtering software or videotape this movie when it airs on television so as to eliminate offensive vocabulary.

Story Summary

In the 1950s, TV quiz shows were all the rage. *The $64,000 Question. Tic Tac Dough. Name That Tune.* Then, in 1958, NBC's *Twenty-One* captured headlines for all the wrong reasons when news broke that contestants were receiving the answers in advance as part of a scam to boost ratings. Nominated for four Oscars including Best Picture, *Quiz Show* is an entertaining, well-acted account of that scandal and the personalities involved.

Herb Stempel hungered for validation. The applause of the audience. The respect of his family. The adoration of everyone in his working-class New York neighborhood. As a contestant on *Twenty-One*, the nerdy 29-year-old was getting it—albeit dishonestly—and winning thousands of dollars. That is, until his ratings plateaued and the sponsor decided it was time for a new face. Producer Dan Enright told Stempel to take a dive—on an easy question no less. Herb complied, but it was more humiliation than his fragile ego could handle. In the months that followed, he stewed in anger, resentment, and jealousy.

Stempel's successor, Charles Van Doren, was the photogenic son of Pulitzer Prize-winning poet Mark Van Doren. Charlie needed validation too. Despite an impressive academic résumé and a teaching position at Columbia University, Charlie lived in the shadow of the Van Doren legacy. Enright and his partner, Al Freedman, saw this clean-cut kid from a prominent family as their ticket to big ratings, and preyed on his weaknesses:

Enright: What if we were to put you on the show and ask you questions that you know, say, the questions that you answered correctly on the test this morning.

Van Doren: I don't follow you . . . I thought the questions were in a bank vault.

Enright: In a way, they are.

Freedman: You wanna win, don't you?

Van Doren: Well, I think I'd really rather try to beat him honestly.

Enright: What's dishonest?

Freedman: When Gregory Peck parachutes behind enemy lines, do you think that's really Gregory Peck?

Enright: That book that Eisenhower wrote—a ghostwriter wrote it. Nobody cares.

At first, Charlie resisted the idea of cheating, but later gave in to it. He compromised. He loved the money. He loved the attention. He loved the fact that he was the hottest thing on TV, a brand-new medium not yet conquered by any other Van Doren.

Enter Richard Goodwin. This ambitious young government investigator picked up the scent of wrongdoing and, seeking a little validation of his own, went after the industry with great zeal ("We're gonna put television on trial. *Television*. Everybody in the country will know about it"). He visited former contestants (few would talk to him) and developed a genuinely friendly relationship with the coy Charlie and his clan. Then he met Stempel, who provided such detailed and incriminating testimony that Richard realized it would be hard to proceed without hurting his friend Charlie in the process. He gave Van Doren the chance to come clean privately, but the reigning champion maintained his innocence, forcing Goodwin to subpoena him.

When the truth finally came out, each of these men suffered collateral damage from his own obsessive quest. Stempel lashed out at NBC and Van Doren, only to worsen his own image and destroy the bond of trust in his marriage. Charlie set out to earn a place among his family's long line of intellectuals, only to tarnish his family name and lose his position at Columbia. And while Goodwin tried to bring TV to its knees, the medium escaped virtually unscathed while an unintended target, the Van Doren family, absorbed the brunt of public embarrassment.

At the film's conclusion, Enright defends his actions, saying, "The sponsor makes out. The network makes out. The contestants see money they probably would never see in a lifetime, and the public is entertained. So who gets hurt?" Integrity. The public trust. And, as *Quiz Show* illustrates in gripping detail, these intangibles are not the *only* casualties when truth and character take a backseat to envy and greed.

Before You Watch

Tune in to a popular TV game show. Talk about the inherent trust viewers must have in the integrity of the game and what might happen if we learned that a contestant had been given the answers in advance. Explain that, if even one person isn't playing by the rules, everyone suffers.

Bible Bookmarks

Prov. 12:22, 22:1; Matt. 4:1-11; Col. 2:8; 1 Thes. 5:21-22; Rom. 12:2; Ps. 101:3; Jdg. 16

Talking Points

1. Discuss the motivations of Van Doren, Stempel, and Goodwin. How was each trying to make a name for himself? What unintended consequences resulted from these quests for personal validation?

2. Dave Garroway tells Charlie, "This is the largest classroom in the world, professor—television." What does he mean? What are the implications today? Apply Colossians 2:8, 1 Thessalonians 5:21-22, Romans 12:2, and Psalm 101:3.

3. Review Charlie's stages of compromise. How did he go from "I would have to say 'no'" to becoming America's most infamous fraud? You can relate this slippery slope to the story of Samson in Judges 16.

4. In his prepared statement, Charlie says, "I've learned that good and evil aren't always what they appear to be." Dissect the ways Enright and Freedman identified Charlie's weaknesses and used subtle lies and rationalizations to gain his cooperation. How does Satan use similar tactics to deceive, and how can a knowledge of Scripture help us defend ourselves? Read Matthew 4:1-11.

5. Examine the complexities of the father/son relationship shared by Charles and Mark Van Doren. It's natural for teens to see the story's dramatic turn of events from the child's perspective. Encourage them to look through the father's eyes. Then compare Mark's character—his love for his son, the pain he feels upon learning of Charlie's sin, and the support he lends following repentance—to our heavenly Father's grace and love.

6. Consider Mark's stinging reminder to Charlie, "Your name is *mine.*" Read Proverbs 22:1 and apply that verse to the tarnishing of the Van Doren family name.

7. After Stempel's wife overhears his confession to Goodwin, she feels betrayed ("I was one of those saps, Herbert"). What does she mean when she asks, "What else did you do that you didn't mention?" Talk about what this type of deception can do to a marriage.

8. Some teens believe cheating is okay if they don't get caught. Goodwin told Charlie about his uncle who confessed to an extramarital affair eight years after the fact. What did he mean when he said, "It's the getting away with it part he couldn't live with"?

9. Stempel's assertion that gentiles regularly beat Jews on the show and earned more money, as well as Goodwin's remarks about the

Reuben sandwich, suggest that anti-Semitism was a problem at that time. Discuss the issue. Then take a closer look at Stempel's own racially charged comments ("uncircumcized putz," "see Charles Van Doren eat his first kosher meal").

10. The producers of *Twenty-One* had an anything-for-ratings mentality. How is that attitude manifested in today's television climate? Give some examples. As consumers of entertainment, what should be our response?

11. What the quiz shows were to the mid-1950s, reality shows have become to the early 21st century. Imagine the fallout if a show like *Survivor* was exposed as being rigged. Would there be the same uproar today that Van Doren faced in 1958? Why or why not? Read Proverbs 12:22 for God's feelings about honesty.

 ## Follow-Up Activity

Research the quiz show scandal on which the film is based. These resources will help:

• PBS's *The American Experience* documentary "The Quiz Show Scandal." For information about the video, a complete transcript, teaching tips, news clippings, etc., log on to www.pbs.org/wgbh/amex/quizshow.

• The book *Prime Time and Misdemeanors: Investigating the 1950's Quiz Scandal: A D.A.'s Account* by Joseph Stone, the district attorney who was lied to by co-conspirators in the *Twenty-One* debacle.

Just for Fun

A sudden ratings boom for one show often means a sharp decline for another. You may be surprised to know that the competition most negatively impacted by Van Doren's 14-week run on *Twenty-One* was CBS's classic sitcom *I Love Lucy*.

—*Bob Smithouser*

Remember the Titans

Rated: PG
Themes: Racism, teamwork, pride, unity, putting aside ambition and jealousy for the greater good, rising above tragic circumstances
Running Time: 1 hour, 54 minutes
Starring: Denzel Washington as Herman Boone; Will Patton as Bill Yoast; Ryan Hurst as Bertier; Wood Harris as Julius; Donald Faison as Petey; Kip Pardue as Sunshine
Directed by: Boaz Yakin

Cautions

A half-dozen mild profanities. Bigots refer to Coach Boone as Coach Coon (the film's most egregious racial slur). During some locker-room shenanigans, a plucky new player plants a kiss on a repulsed Bertier, which leads to speculation about the boy's sexual preference.

Story Summary

Peter Schneider, former chairman of Walt Disney Studios, described his introduction to *Remember the Titans* as follows: "[Producer] Jerry Bruckheimer brought it to me and I said, 'Take out all the swear words.' In the script, every third word was the n-word, every fourth word was the f-word, and every sixth word was the s-word." Not anymore. What remains is an inspirational film suitable for family viewing. It's the true story of a city ravaged by racism in 1971, the newly integrated football team at the epicenter of the tension, and how those athletes eventually overcame prejudice to unite the community.

Redistricting turns lily-white TC Williams high school of Alexandria,

Virginia, into a melting pot of flesh tones. Aggravating things further, Herman Boone, a black journeyman football coach from North Carolina, is handed the head coaching position, displacing beloved white coach Bill Yoast in a case of affirmative action. Most whites in Alexandria find it unfair, while the black residents cheer Boone's presence. Yoast, tempted to leave the school, humbly accepts a demotion in hopes of protecting "his boys." After receiving a chilly reception from Coach Yoast and white students protecting their turf, Boone promises that "the best player will play; color won't matter." However, that assurance isn't enough to earn the confidence of white players or ease the anger and distrust the black athletes feel toward their white teammates.

Boone's coaching ability is immediately tested when the Titans head out of town for preseason training camp. Infighting inhibits the team's progress. Then a turning point occurs when Boone escorts his team to a gravesite from the Battle of Gettysburg where he delivers a persuasive speech on unity. The team realizes that winning is contingent upon how well they cooperate. As the camp reaches its end, players bond over Motown tunes and friendships begin to form, especially between defensive leaders Bertier and Julius. The Titans return to Alexandria ready to fight for the state championship.

Another fundamental clash involves the coaching styles of Boone and Yoast. Boone is an ambitious drill sergeant less concerned about his players' enjoyment of the game than their mastery of his pared-down playbook. His word is law. He refuses to tolerate failure and isn't above humiliating undisciplined athletes. Yoast, on the other hand, has a soft spot for trick plays and is quick to protect his players' self-esteem.

Boone: You think you're doing these boys a favor taking 'em aside every time I come down on 'em—protectin' 'em from big bad Boone. You're cuttin' my legs from under me.

Yoast: Some of the boys just don't respond well to public criticism. I tell them what they need to know, but I don't humiliate them in front of the team.

Boone: . . . I may be a mean cuss, but I'm the same mean cuss with everybody out there on that football field. . . . You ain't doing these kids a favor by patronizing 'em. You're crippling 'em. You're crippling 'em for life.

Despite winning their first game against the Hayfield Hawks, the Titans still must battle racist attitudes in the community (someone throws a rock through Boone's living room window) and occasional division amongst themselves (a bigoted blocker intentionally lets a defender flatten his black quarterback). Meanwhile, Boone learns that losing a single game will cost him his job. In fact, a pivotal game finds the referees instructed to cheat so that the Titans will lose, only to have Yoast stand up against the fix, jeopardizing his pending hall-of-fame induction in an attempt to do the right thing.

Tragedy strikes the club just before the state championship. Bertier is paralyzed from the waist down in a car accident. It's a bittersweet turn of events. While Bertier—who refuses to wallow in self-pity—finds himself permanently sidelined, the crisis shows us how close Bertier and Julius have grown, and how Bertier's mother and girlfriend have learned to let go of racial prejudice. After the Titans overcome a half-time deficit to win the championship, Yoast and Boone hoist the game ball together as Boone tells his partner, "You're a hall-of-famer in my book!"

Before You Watch

Christian music as far back as "Jesus Loves the Little Children" has taught young people that God views everyone equally, regardless of skin color. A wonderful modern example is "Colored People," a song by dc Talk, whose title refers to the broad spectrum of skin tones that make up the human race (it appears on the trio's CDs *Jesus Freak, Intermission: The Greatest Hits* and *Welcome to the Freak Show*, and on the CCM compilation project *WOW 1998*). Lines include, "This thing of beauty is the passion of an artist's heart./By God's design, we are a skin kaleidoscope." Listen to the musical recording "Colored People" and read through its smart lyrics together as a primer for the racial issues you'll face in the film.

Bible Bookmarks
Gal. 3:26-29; Eph. 4:1-16; 1 Cor. 1:10; Rom. 1:26-27, 8:28;
Lev. 18:22; Acts 3-4

Talking Points

1. In Acts chapters 3 and 4, we see the quiet, contemplative John paired with the bold, tactless Peter. Obviously, God sees value in teaming unlike personalities. How does this compare with the tense partnership between Boone and Yoast? In life, what are some other ways God uses opposites to overcome differences and complement each other?

2. Have you ever been teamed with someone who was so unlike you that you wondered if you would be able to work with that person? What if that person hated you? How would you handle it? Would you retreat or work it out? How have you handled situations like this in the past?

3. Coach Boone tells his players, "We will be perfect in every aspect of the game." Why is being well-rounded in skill and discipline important? How does that relate to our spiritual lives?

4. Imagine a world without racial diversity. Would there still be conflict? Why or why not? Introduce Galatians 3:26-29 and Ephesians 4:1-16 as calls to Christian unity.

5. Sunshine seems to be joking around when he plants a kiss on Bertier. But what if he's not? How does God feel about homosexuality (Leviticus 18:22, Romans 1:26-27)? While we are called to "hate the sin and love the sinner," why is homosexuality not an issue of accepting diversity?

6. Contrast the coaching styles and motivational tactics of Boone and Yoast. Which do you respect more and why? Have you known or played for a coach like either of these men? Talk about that.

7. Coach Yoast has his position taken away on the basis of race. Do you think it was right to consider race in this situation? Why or why not? What do you think influenced Coach Yoast's decision to put aside bitterness, jealousy, and selfish ambition for the good of the team?

8. Following his accident, Bertier tells Yoast, "Y'know, I've been reading up on the activities they've got for people in wheelchairs and such. They got olympics." Do you think he was feeling sorry for himself? Read Romans 8:28 and discuss how Christians are uniquely equipped to resist self-pity and gain perspective on tragedy.

9. References to Christianity appear throughout the story. Talk about the scores and fumbles in the film's varied portrayals of people of faith. (Examples range from self-righteous bigotry by religious people to players singing gospel songs and respecting "Rev.")

10. Talk about Boone's statement in the graveyard, "Hatred destroyed my family. You listen and take a lesson from the dead. If we don't come together, right now on this hallowed ground, we too will be destroyed just like they were. I don't care if you like each other or not, but you will respect each other." What did he mean?

Follow-Up Activity

Introduce teens to modern-day heroes of the faith who have suffered physical tragedies, as Bertier did, and have emerged victorious. Two shining examples are paraplegic author, speaker, and artist Joni Eareckson Tada (visit www.joniandfriends.org), and former major league baseball player Dave Dravecky, whose career was cut short by cancer and the eventual amputation of his pitching arm (www.dravecky.org). Both Joni and Dave have turned their disabilities into opportunities for God to use them in His service.

Just for Fun

Observant football fans may notice a goof at the end of the Titans' first victory. The game-winning touchdown comes when a Hayfield receiver is tackled, coughs up the ball, and a Titan runs it in for the score. One problem: The Titan player doesn't reverse field. He takes it into the wrong end zone. Oops

—*Bob Smithouser*

Searching for Bobby Fischer

Rated: PG
Themes: Preserving decency and innocence in a cutthroat world, developing one's gifts, sportsmanship, the father-son bond
Running Time: 1 hour, 51 minutes
Starring: Max Pomerance as Josh Waitzkin; Joe Mantegna as Fred Waitzkin; Joan Allen as Bonnie Waitzkin; Ben Kingsley as Bruce Pandolfini; Laurence Fishburne as Vinnie
Directed by: Steven Zaillian

 ## Cautions
Two misuses of the Lord's name.

 ## Story Summary
Searching for Bobby Fischer opens to black-and-white newsreel footage of America's most famous chess player, overdubbed with biographical insights by a young boy. The child explains that, after becoming world champion in 1972, Fischer made his most unexpected move of all . . . *he disappeared*. No one knew where he was or why he had chosen a life of seclusion. Years went by. No Bobby Fischer. The movie's cryptic title alludes to two searches. First, the chess community continually had its eyes open for Fischer in the form of a talented stranger who might wander into a pickup game and display his signature, grand-master panache. At another level, it reflects the search

for Fischer's heir apparent, that gifted prodigy who might become the *next* world-class phenom.

However, this true story isn't about Bobby Fischer. It's not really even about chess. It's about a seven-year-old boy with a special gift, and how his exceptionally kind *heart* impacted various adults in his life who had their own ideas about how to hone his talent.

After seeing men playing speed chess in the park, Josh Waitzkin becomes enthralled. Pawns. Knights. Rooks. Bishops. It becomes a new interest on his long list of play-time activities. But those around him quickly realize he has an uncanny head for the game. His devoted father, Fred (who wrote the book on which the film is based), is committed to helping Josh excel. That includes hiring a classically trained tutor named Bruce Pandolfini, a strict mentor who knows the amateur circuit, including what it can do to promising young minds that aren't properly trained to win. Making Bruce's job more difficult is Vinnie, a homeless man who encourages Josh's love for "speed chess," a variation Bruce eschews as the game's undisciplined evil twin. In the midst of this ideological tug-of-war, Josh's mother pledges to do whatever it takes to preserve her son's sweet spirit in this take-no-prisoners subculture obsessed with winning ("He's not weak," she tells Fred, "he's decent. And if you or Bruce or anyone else tries to beat that out of him . . . I'll take him away"). She needn't worry. The boy knows who he is . . . and who he's not:

Bruce: Do you know what the word contempt means? It's to think of them as being beneath you, to be unworthy of being in the same room with you.

Josh: I don't feel that.

Bruce: Well, you'd better start, because if you don't think it's a part of winning, you're wrong. You have to have contempt for your opponent. You have to hate them.

Josh: But I don't.

Bruce: They hate you. (Josh shrugs.) They hate you, Josh.

Josh: But I don't hate them.

Bruce: Bobby Fischer held the world in contempt.

Josh: I'm not him.

Bruce: You're telling me.

In the months and tournaments that follow, Josh experiences a series of ups and downs. He takes the chess world by storm, then struggles with the pressure of being ranked number one. Inexplicable losses put stress on Josh's relationship with his dad, forcing both to refocus on what's most important. Along the way, Josh meets Jonathan, an intimidating child prodigy whose ability is equalled only by his smug, rude demeanor. "He's been my student since he was four," his teacher boasts. "His parents have given him to me. He does nothing but play chess. No other interests." Quite a contrast to young Waitzkin. Eventually, Josh and Jonathan face off in a climactic battle. Of course, Josh wins, but it's *how* he wins that will put a lump in viewers' throats. And through it all, Josh's kind-hearted nature emerges unscathed.

No knowledge of chess is required to enjoy *Searching for Bobby Fischer*, though it doesn't hurt. At its core, the story is about one family's emotional journey. Yes, Josh Waitzkin is a brilliant chess player. More importantly, he's a decent, sensitive, merciful competitor. Because the film emphasizes the latter, this under-appreciated gem embodies the warmth, innocence, and virtue of its young hero.

Before You Watch

If you and your teen enjoy chess, play a day or two before you view the film (since games can run long, combining a game with the movie and discussion could be too much for one evening). Taking time to survey the board, handle the pieces, and form strategy can prepare teens to better relate to Josh's world.

Bible Bookmarks

2 Pet. 1:7; Matt. 5:7; Rom. 12:14-16; Ex. 20:12; Prov. 18:3; Jer. 48:29; Mk. 8:34-36; Eph. 6:4

Talking Points

1. Discuss how Josh's words and deeds reveal a good heart and reflect biblical virtues. How does Josh show kindness (2 Peter 1:7), mercy (Matthew 5:7), empathy (Romans 12:14-16), and respect for his parents (Exodus 20:12)? Talk about how he refuses to arrogantly hold others in contempt (Proverbs 18:3, Jeremiah 48:29).

2. Bruce worried that speed chess would undermine the structured method he was trying to teach Josh, yet the boy's ultimate victory came from drawing upon *both*. How does this ability to be disciplined *and* boldly spontaneous relate to the Christian life?

3. Talk about Vinnie's statement, "You're playing not to lose, Josh. You've got to risk everything. You've got to go to the edge of defeat." Relate it to Jesus' words in Mark 8:34-36. Why do you think people are so often tempted to hold back and not put everything on the line, be it in matters of religious faith, romantic love, or the pursuit of personal success?

4. How do the members of the Waitzkin family honor and love one another? Share some examples together, and be sure to praise teens when one gets mentioned that *they* happen to be very good at as well.

5. Ephesians 6:4 warns, "Fathers, do not exasperate your children." How can overly competitive parents like Morgan's dad exasperate their children? What would be a healthier approach for parents to take?

6. What does our culture value most in athletes, "winning" or "character"? What evidence have you encountered that supports your claim? Why do you think this is the case?

7. What is our responsibility to our God-given gifts? Does a math genius have the obligation to pursue rocket science? Is a biology whiz bound by social duty to work at curing cancer? How does this relate to *spiritual* gifts?

8. There are so many interesting characters in this film, it's a great opportunity to develop a sense of empathy by having teens step back and view events through the eyes of various supporting players. Also ask, "With which character do you most identify? Why?"

9. Contrast Josh's varied interests with the obsessive single-mindedness of Jonathan. Which do you think is healthier? Why?

10. Look closely at the relationship between Josh and his dad. In what ways do they see the "chess thing" (as Josh's teacher calls it) differently? How do father and son grow to understand, respect, and love each other more deeply through it all?

11. Jonathan's tutor tells Bruce, "There are only so many things you can teach a child, and finally, they are who they are." What did he mean by that? Do you agree?

Follow-Up Activity

Attend an athletic event featuring competitors under the age of 10 (soccer, football, baseball, etc.). The nature of the sport isn't important. You're there to listen to the parents and coaches, specifically how they handle the young players. Are they supportive? Do they lack perspective? Do you hear hypercompetitive parents living through their children? Afterward, talk about what you witnessed and compare the people you encountered to the "chess parents" in the movie.

Just for Fun

Here's a little-known film fact. Despite winning critical raves and boasting an all-star cast, *Searching for Bobby Fischer* vanished from theaters after only three weeks on a paltry 219 screens. It was basically abandoned by its studio (Paramount) which, coincidentally, released the bloody horror sequel *Jason Goes to Hell: The Final Friday* that very same weekend (August 13, 1993) on a whopping 1,355 screens. Even when Hollywood manages to create a family film of substance, the system sometimes fails to support it.

—*Bob Smithouser*

Sense and Sensibility

Rated: PG
Themes: Using one's head vs. heart in love and courtship, loyalty, modesty, the riches of good character, keeping wealth and status in perspective
Running Time: 2 hours, 16 minutes
Starring: Emma Thompson as Elinor Dashwood; Kate Winslet as Marianne Dashwood; Hugh Grant as Edward Ferrars; Alan Rickman as Colonel Brandon; Gemma Jones as Mrs. Dashwood; Greg Wise as John Willoughby
Directed by: Ang Lee

Cautions

Aside from two uses of "good God," language is pristine. In fact, *Sense and Sensibility* is a very innocent film appropriate for teens of any age, though its unhurried pace and poetic dialogue may challenge younger adolescents.

Story Summary

Glorious scenery, crack-shot acting, subtle humor, and strong family values make the 1996 Oscar and Golden Globe winner *Sense and Sensibility* a stunning adaptation of Jane Austen's novel. The story opens in rural England in the early 1800s. As the elder Mr. Dashwood lies dying, he informs John (his son from his first marriage) that legal issues prevent him from dividing his estate between his two families. His second wife and three daughters will be left poor if John doesn't help them. But John's initial resolve to provide for his family is slowly whittled away by his selfish and annoyingly haughty wife, Fanny. Fanny's meddling leaves the Dashwood women homeless, penniless, and dowry-less.

Adversity leads to the development of terrific feminine characters. The endearing Dashwoods struggle with the constraints placed on them by their loss of wealth and social status. Moreover, when the two eldest fall in love with eligible bachelors, their wildly different approaches to matters of the heart provide delicious food for thought. The hopelessly romantic Marianne is a fun-loving free spirit. Her older sister, Elinor, is more reserved, proper, and analytical.

Level-headed Elinor's affections are captured by the chivalrous and lovably insecure Edward Ferrars, an heir to wealth and high position who would rather lead a humble parish in the country than rub shoulders with the social elite. In contrast, Marianne becomes infatuated with John Willoughby, a handsome rogue who rescues her after she takes a nasty fall in the rain. He quotes Shakespeare with passionate inflection, delivers handpicked wildflower bouquets, and has a playful sense of humor. Both suitors are unexpectedly called away. The Dashwood women are left to the company of their country relatives (including a match-making busybody) and Colonel Brandon, a kindhearted nobleman with a sad past who adores Marianne but doesn't stand a chance against the dashing Willoughby.

A generous relative invites Marianne and Elinor to London, where things get emotionally complicated for the sisters. Elinor is informed that Edward has been secretly engaged to Lucy Steele for five years. Meanwhile, Willoughby has dropped out of sight and won't return Marianne's messages. Nothing is quite what it seems. We learn that Willoughby's past indiscretions are forcing him to marry another woman for her money, and that Edward is battling between true love and a sense of obligation. Indeed, both Elinor's stoicism and Marianne's ardor get buffeted by the waves of courtship. In the end, their love for each other and for their future husbands is refined, and Austen tips her hat to romantic justice on the path to "happily ever after."

Before You Watch

Dads with daughters: Don't just watch a movie; plan an evening. If father/daughter dates are already a family tradition—or if you'd like to make them one—be a true gentleman and take your daughter to dinner. Treat her like a queen. Talk about how she expects to be treated by young men in friendship or dating situations.

Discuss the movie's title. Today, "sense" and "sensibility" can be taken to mean almost the same thing. When Jane Austen wrote this novel, the latter denoted "sensitivity" or an inclination to strong emotion. Being clued in to this etymological trivia helps us understand the contrast between Elinor and Marianne.

Familiarize teens with the concept of a "dowry," the practice of a bride's family giving money or possessions to the groom as a part of the marriage agreement. Ask them how they feel about that concept.

Bible Bookmarks

Prov. 12:4, 19:13-14, 20:6-7; 1 Cor. 13:7-8; Jas. 2:1-9; Matt. 6:19-21; Rom. 6:23; Ex. 34:6-7; Ps. 37:30, 100:5; Gal. 5:22-23; Eph. 5:25-28; Col. 4:5-6

Talking Points

1. John Dashwood fully intends to support his stepmother and half sisters until Fanny talks him out of it. Read Proverbs 12:4 and 19:13-14. If you'd had the opportunity to speak to John before he married Fanny, what advice would you have given him?

2. What kinds of first impressions do Edward, Colonel Brandon, and Willoughby make? Do these impressions turn out to be accurate representations of their character? What can we learn from this? Can you recall a first impression that missed the mark? If so, explain.

3. Describe Fanny's attitude toward wealth and status. How does this line up with what the Bible says in James 2:1-9 and Matthew 6:19-21? Which characters suffer because others take this attitude? Who in the

film better exhibits a godly perspective? How?

4. Marianne and Elinor make several statements throughout the film exposing their differing views of love:

Marianne: To love is to burn, to be on fire . . . To die for love. What could be more glorious?

Elinor: In certain situations, perhaps it's better to use one's head.

Marianne: But Elinor, your heart must tell you . . .

Elinor: I do not attempt to deny that I think very highly of him . . . that I greatly esteem him . . . I like him.

Marianne: Esteem him? Like him? Use those insipid words again and I shall leave the room this instant.

With which do you identify more? Cite beneficial and detrimental aspects of each approach. What happens when our view of love is unbalanced—either all head or all heart? During the course of the story, what do Marianne and Elinor learn from each other?

5. "Love is not love/Which alters when it alteration finds/Or bends with the remover to remove/O no, it is an ever fixéd mark/That looks on tempests and is never shaken." Paraphrase this Shakespearean sonnet (# 116) that Marianne and Willoughby read together. How does it parallel 1 Corinthians 13:7-8 and Psalm 100:5?

6. Even though Mrs. Jennings is a chatterbox, Margaret says, "I like her. She *talks* about things. We never talk about things." What does she mean? Do you feel there are difficult issues your family needs to talk about that get ignored? What are they?

7. In contrast, Mrs. Dashwood tells her youngest, "If you can't think of anything appropriate to say, you will kindly restrict your remarks to the weather." Are there times when it's appropriate or even necessary to be extra-discreet about our conversation? When and why? How does Colossians 4:5-6 apply?

8. For all we can tell, Willoughby truly loves Marianne, but his past actions catch up with him and prevent him from marrying her. Do you think he learns his lesson in the end? What can he teach us about sin's consequences? Check out Exodus 34:6-7 and Romans 6:23.

9. For all of its giddiness and passion on the subject of romantic love, this film doesn't glorify sex. There's not even so much as a kiss. Yet with modesty, anticipation can create even greater emotions. With that in mind, discuss the following quote by 21st-century columnist Mona Charen: "You cannot experience the thrill of a first kiss when you've heard and seen everything long before you're ready. If the counterrevolu-

tion against the sexual revolution is to be won, it will not be fear of AIDS or pregnancy that will tip the balance. It will be a longing for the excitement, the mystery and the sweetness, which has youthful innocence as its prerequisite."

10. Edward Ferrars and Colonel Brandon turn out to be the story's true gentlemen. What character traits qualify them as such? What does the Bible say about these qualities? (Try Psalm 37:30, Proverbs 20:6-7, Galatians 5:22-23, and Ephesians 5:25-28 for starters.) Ask teens what qualities they're looking for in a potential mate and ask, "How can I help you keep your standards high?"

11. Which character struck you as being most like yourself? Which one did you find most likable? Were there any that really rubbed you the wrong way? Offer specific reasons to support your answers.

Follow-Up Activity

In recent years, many Jane Austen works have been translated to film *(Sense and Sensibility, Emma, Persuasion, Pride and Prejudice, Mansfield Park)*. Learn more about the woman responsible for these 19th-century stories of romance and English propriety. Biographical information can be found at www.pemberley. com/janeinfo/janelife.html.

Just for Fun

Even Oscar-caliber motion pictures can include mistakes. When Lucy leans over to confide in Fanny, she's holding a small dog in her lap. The shot widens mere seconds later as Fanny erupts, but the dog is nowhere in sight. Oops!

—Lindy Beam

Sergeant York

Not Rated
Themes: Spiritual redemption, perseverance, integrity, the tension of honoring both God and country, wartime heroism
Running Time: 2 hours, 14 minutes
Starring: Gary Cooper as Alvin York; Walter Brennan as Pastor Pile; Joan Leslie as Gracie Williams
Directed by: Howard Hawks

Cautions

Violent WWI combat shows men dying on the battlefield, victims of mortar shells, hand grenades, machine-gun fire, bayonets, etc. (one brief shot shows a man bleeding from the mouth, but no other deaths are graphic). An unredeemed Alvin gets drunk and into fistfights.

Story Summary

Deep in the heart of Tennessee's Cumberland Mountains in 1916, earth-workin' country folk sing "When the Roll Is Called Up Yonder." Their graying pastor speaks from Luke 15 on the parable of the lost sheep. Then shots ring out. It seems several local "lost sheep" have had too much to drink and are whooping it up outside, being so disruptive that the pastor sends everyone home. The lead carouser is Alvin York, eldest son of a lady in the church. Soon after, at the general store also run by Pastor Pile, Mother York asks the minister to speak with her prodigal. He agrees, and finds Alvin plowing his fields:

Alvin: Sorry about the other night. I reckon I done the wrong thing.

Pastor: Y'see that rock, Alvin? You been plowin' around that rock a heap o' years.

Alvin: Sure have.

Pastor: Did you ever think when you start plowin' your furrows crooked it's mighty hard to get 'em straight again?

Alvin: I never thought on it much.

Pastor: Well, it's that way, I reckon— with other things besides plowin'.

He tells Alvin that Satan has him by the shirttail, and talks about a man's need for roots in something outside of himself. Alvin respect-fully shares his belief that a fella doesn't go lookin' for religion; it's got to find him.

Of course, Alvin isn't entirely without vision. He's smitten with Gracie and wants to marry her. Trouble is, she seems interested in Zeb, presumably because Zeb owns "bottom land." You see, Alvin farms "top land," which is rockier, harder to work, and less fruitful. He figures scoring a piece of bottom land could change things. So Alvin sells most of his belongings and labors for two months (toting rocks, splitting rails, felling trees) to buy a plot of land. At dead-line, he's a bit short, but convinces the man holding the deed to extend him a few days so he can win the balance at a turkey shoot. He wins, only to learn that the property has already been sold to Zeb.

Alvin responds by getting drunk. Then he rides off, rifle in hand, to take revenge. But before he can do something he'll regret, he has a Damascus Road experience. Lightning knocks him off his horse and destroys his gun. Scared straight, Alvin enters the church, walks to the front, and hits his knees.

Alvin York is a changed man. He teaches children the Bible, fully confident in its authority. He shows forgiveness to those who've wronged him. He even has a different attitude about fighting. In fact, when local men are forced to register for the draft, he seeks an exemption as a con-scientious objector ("I ain't a'goin' to war. War is killin'. And the Book's agin killin'. So war is agin the Book"). Still, it's the law so Alvin signs up, confident that the draft board will honor an appeal. He and Gracie plan their future. But Uncle Sam has other ideas.

At boot camp, Alvin endures snide remarks from a sergeant who learns he tried to avoid service. However, people's attitudes change when Alvin proves to be an *unbelievable* marksman. He turns down a promotion, which leads to an interesting dialogue between Alvin and sympathetic officers who explain the need to defend our freedoms, religious and otherwise. He's given a brief furlough to think it over. In the familiar hills of Tennessee, he reads from a history book and the Bible, and wrestles with his duties to God and country. Mark 12:17 convinces him that he should go to war.

During WWI's Meuse-Argonne offensive, Alvin sees scores of men killed by the Germans. His platoon is pinned down and woefully outnumbered. Alvin leaps into action and picks off several nests full of machine gunners, then forces an entire enemy unit to surrender and, along with seven other American survivors, marches 132 prisoners into custody. From conscientious objector to war hero, Alvin York is highly decorated, yet remains humble. His greatest reward is that coveted piece of bottom land and the chance to live out the American dream with the girl he loves.

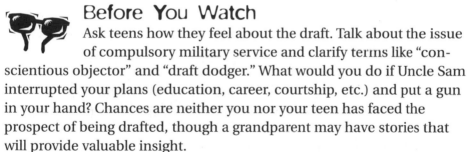

Before You Watch

Ask teens how they feel about the draft. Talk about the issue of compulsory military service and clarify terms like "conscientious objector" and "draft dodger." What would you do if Uncle Sam interrupted your plans (education, career, courtship, etc.) and put a gun in your hand? Chances are neither you nor your teen has faced the prospect of being drafted, though a grandparent may have stories that will provide valuable insight.

Bible Bookmarks

1 Thes. 5:14-15; Matt. 5:14-16, 5:23-24, 7:7-11, 18:21-35; Gen. 29:13-30; Jas. 2:14-26;1 Pet. 5:5; Mk. 12:17

Talking Points

1. York and his commanding officers have a rich conversation about freedom and the need to defend it. Talk about

that exchange. What is our responsibility—as Christians and as a nation—to intercede in conflict? Read 1 Thessalonians 5:14-15. If people like Alvin York hadn't battled evil in World Wars I and II, what might have happened to the Jews and other targets of genocide?

2. What did Pastor Pile mean when he used "plowing furrows" as an analogy for staying on the straight and narrow? Is there an area of *your* life where bad habits are getting harder to straighten out the longer they're left unchallenged?

3. Alvin doesn't believe a man should actively seek spiritual things. How does that philosophy contradict Jesus' words in Matthew 7:7-11? Take a moment to share your testimony or ask teens to share theirs.

4. Ask teens how they felt when Zeb ended up with the land Alvin worked so hard to obtain. Why was this so unfair? In Genesis 29:13-30, we learn about how Laban took unfair advantage of Jacob. Read that passage, then ask teens if anyone has ever cheated them. How did they respond? If it were to happen again, how might they handle it differently?

5. How does Alvin's forgiving spirit prove he was a changed man? Read James 2:14-26 and discuss the connection between a person's faith and his actions. Why must we let our "light shine before men" as described in Matthew 5:14-16? Pastor Pile does so quietly by offering Alvin a fair price for a fox pelt after others took advantage of his desperate situation. Do you think this factored into Alvin's decision to turn his life over to God? Why or why not?

6. Read Jesus' commands regarding reconciliation (Matthew 5:23-24) and forgiveness (Matthew 18:21-35). Instead of simmering in bitterness, Alvin humbly approaches those who wronged him. How can we resist the temptation to lash out at those who hurt us?

7. Pastor Pile tells Alvin, "You got the *usin'* kind of religion, not the *meetin'-house* kind." What did he mean? What can we do to make sure we've got the usin' kind of faith and not just the kind people show off on Sunday morning?

8. A great stressor in a marriage is unfulfilled expectations. Why do you think that's such an issue? Gracie's expectations were simple: "I expect my husband to love me. I reckon the good Lord will take care of the rest." Do you think that attitude is healthy, or is it overly simplistic? Why?

9. After the war, Alvin may be decorated with medals, but he's *clothed* with humility (1 Peter 5:5). He turns down $250,000 in endorse-

ments because he says his heroics were part of a job and "ain't for buyin' and sellin'." Would it have been wrong to take the money? Why or why not? Ask teens what they would have done if placed in that situation.

Follow-Up Activity

Alvin York isn't a Hollywood concoction, but a real man who did the things portrayed onscreen. Teens wanting to know more about him, including what happened in the years leading up to and following the movie's release, should visit http://volweb.utk.edu/Schools/York/history.html.

A sobering thought: *Sergeant York* opened nationwide on September 27, 1941, mere weeks before the Japanese attack on Pearl Harbor thrust America into the Second World War. Mention this to teens, and pause to consider that many of the heroic men whose deaths in WWII would later be portrayed in *other* Hollywood epics—from *The Longest Day* to *Saving Private Ryan*—watched the very same movie you've just shared together mere months before giving their lives for their country.

Just for Fun

What's a life story worth? In the case of Alvin York, Warner Bros. reportedly paid him $169,449.84. York used the money to pay off his debts. He was quoted in the *Farm Credit Manager* as saying, "I'll bet I'm the first person who ever paid off a Federal Land Bank loan with money from a movie."

—Bob Smithouser

Shadowlands

Rated: PG
Themes: God's role in suffering, risking pain for intimacy, intellectual integrity, romantic love in marriage
Running Time: 2 hours, 13 minutes
Starring: Anthony Hopkins as C.S. Lewis; Debra Winger as Joy Gresham; Edward Hardwicke as Warnie; Joseph Mazzello as Douglas
Directed by: Richard Attenborough

Cautions

The Lewis brothers smoke pipes. Despite alluding to the consequences of alcoholism, the film features social drinking in many scenes (the local pub is a favorite hangout for the Oxford elite). Some might object to Jack's use of the term "bloody awful."

Story Summary

Shadowlands chronicles the budding friendship and romance shared by English author and Christian apologist C.S. "Jack" Lewis and Joy Gresham, the transplanted New York poet who captured his heart in the early 1950s before she succumbed to cancer.

We meet Jack as an aging bachelor enjoying a proper, undisturbed life as a professor at Oxford University. He lives with his brother, Warnie. A well-known writer, Jack speaks publicly and spars intellectually with peers at a local pub. Jack has much to say about grief and suffering, and is accused by one colleague of supplying "easy answers to difficult questions." During one lecture, he quotes a letter he received in which the writer, referring to a tragic accident that took 24 innocent lives, asks Lewis, "Where was God? Why didn't He stop it? Isn't God supposed to be

141

good? Isn't He supposed to love us? Does God want us to suffer?" He replies, "I suggest to you that it is *because* God loves us that He makes us the gift of suffering. Pain is God's megaphone to rouse a deaf world."

Jack's calm, emotionally aloof world is altered when he agrees to have tea with visiting American Joy Gresham, a fan who has been corresponding with him. He anticipates an "hour or so of polite conversation, then we go home and everything goes on just the way it always has." But that initial meeting turns into a tour of Oxford, more teas, a Christmas dinner, and the acquaintance of Joy's young son, Douglas. Through it all, Joy's enchantingly brazen ability to challenge Jack in matters of philosophy becomes a central source of attraction:

Jack: Personal experience isn't everything.

Joy: I disagree. I think personal experience is everything.

Jack: So, reading is a waste of time?

Joy: No, it's not a waste of time. But reading is "safe," isn't it? Books aren't about to hurt you.

Jack: Why should one want to be hurt?

Joy: That's when we learn.

It seems Joy's journey to England was partly to escape the abuse of her alcoholic, "compulsively unfaithful" husband. Joy asks only for Jack's friendship, which he gladly offers. When Joy returns to America, Jack attempts to ignore the void in his life. He thinks of her often and misses their spirited dialogues. After her divorce, Joy moves to London. Jack is delighted to have his friend back and, at her request, marries her so that she can become a citizen. It's a technical union before the state, not before God. No passion. No intimacy. It's a platonic arrangement between friends, allowing Jack to keep his comfortably cloistered heart "safe."

Soon after, Joy is stricken with cancer. Faced with losing her, Jack realizes how deeply he loves her and asks to marry her again, this time in the eyes of God. Their remaining months together are filled with a true, strong, emotionally intimate romance. When Joy dies, Jack and Douglas both have their worlds torn asunder—forever altered by love. Not only has Jack's perfect world shattered, but so has his view of pain and suffering. The man who once had all the answers has nothing left but questions. "Why love if losing hurts so much?" he asks. Yet the viewer senses that, in spite of his frustration, Jack is not only glad for the choice he made to love Joy, but that he is a much deeper, richer, wiser man *and* teacher because of it.

If there's a weakness in this Oscar-nominated film, it's that *Shadowlands* ends with the audience wondering just how severely C.S. Lewis' loss impacted his faith. A more appropriate epilogue would've shown Jack returning from his valley of despair to a renewed and energized relationship with God. That's how his biography really ended. Instead, this articulate saint's conversion and conviction play only a supporting role in what is an otherwise terrific movie. Shortly after its release, the real Douglas Gresham—a committed Christian—said of his stepfather, "Her death taught him something. He had yet to learn that in the very deepest despair there is hope, and when by grief the entire universe is suddenly emptied, there is God."

Before You Watch

C.S. Lewis' personality heavily favored intellect over emotion, which explains why he dealt with circumstances the way he did. Do you know how you and your teen are "wired"? If you've never taken such an inventory, consider doing so. Dr. John Trent's ministry, StrongFamilies.com, offers an online personality examination (http://www.encouragingwords.com/insights.htm).

Bible Bookmarks

Is. 41:10, 43:1-2, 53:3-7; 1 Thes. 5:17; Matt. 6:5-13; Prov. 14:13; 2 Cor. 1:3-5; 1 Pet. 1:6-7; Jas. 1:2-4; Ps. 126:6; Rom. 8:18; Rev. 21:4

Talking Points

1. Lewis preaches, "If you love someone, you don't want them to suffer. You can't bear it. You want to take their suffering on yourself. Even I feel like that. Why doesn't God?" The great romance of the gospel proves that God *did* feel like that and sent His Son

to bear our suffering, as prophesied in Isaiah 53:3-7 and fulfilled in Jesus Christ. Discuss this passage and God's wonderful love.

2. Do you think Jack did the right thing when he married Joy to give her British citizenship? Why or why not? At what point did you sense that Jack was falling in love with her? When did you realize that Joy loved him? How was their marriage healthier after their *second* set of vows?

3. What were your early impressions of Jack? Did they change as the story progressed? Would you consider Joy a good mother? What does she do that shows how much she loves Douglas?

4. When Joy is ill, Jack explains to his friends, "I pray because the need flows out of me all the time, waking and sleeping. It doesn't change God; it changes me." Read 1 Thessalonians 5:17 and Jesus' view of prayer in Matthew 6:5-13. Talk about these perspectives. Why do *you* pray?

5. Jack asks, "Why love if losing hurts so much?" What would you tell him? What would Jack have missed had he *not* opened his heart to Joy? Why do you think he did it? Refer back to the dialogue reprinted in the story summary. Are *you* more inclined to play it safe or boldly step out in this area with friends and loved ones? Why?

6. This isn't your typical cinematic love story. Contrast Hollywood's obsession with perfect storybook romances and "happily ever after" endings to Jack's painful, sacrificial, yet deeply satisfying love for Joy.

7. Jack concludes, "The pain *now* is part of the happiness *then*. That's the deal." Talk about that in light of Proverbs 14:13.

8. What is the point of suffering, and where is God when we endure trials? Clear answers await in 2 Corinthians 1:3-5, 1 Peter 1:6-7, James 1:2-4, and Isaiah 41:10 and 43:1-2.

9. Some hard times last longer than others. Some seem as if they'll last forever. What does God's Word say about the duration of suffering? What is a healthy eternal perspective on it? Read Psalm 126:6, Romans 8:18, and Revelation 21:4.

10. What did Jack mean when he told his students, "The most intense joy lies not in the having, but in the desiring"? Do you agree? Why or why not?

Follow-Up Activity

One of C.S. Lewis' most popular books, *The Screwtape Letters*, analyzes spiritual warfare via correspondences between an apprentice demon and his skilled uncle. Each entry describes ways the forces of evil seek to undermine the spiritual well-being of the humans they're charged with crippling. It's a good one to read through for daily devotions. You could make it a point to discuss each day's reading together either as a family or simply with your teen.

Focus on the Family Radio Theater has faithfully adapted C.S. Lewis' beloved *Chronicles of Narnia* series into compelling audio dramas available on either CD or cassette. At home or on the road, they offer teens a dynamic way to experience Lewis' delightful allegorical fantasies. For more information, call Focus on the Family at 800-232-6459.

Just for Fun

Richard Attenborough, the film's director, may be best known to young people in his role as John Hammond, the grandfatherly theme-park owner responsible for the genetically engineered dinosaurs in *Jurassic Park*. Joseph Mazzello, cast here as Douglas Gresham, played Attenborough's grandson in *Jurassic Park*.

—Lissa Johnson

To Kill a Mockingbird

Not Rated
Themes: Racial prejudice, stereotypes, integrity, treating others with dignity, standing for truth despite opposition
Running Time: 2 hours, 9 minutes
Starring: Gregory Peck as Atticus Finch; Mary Badham as Jean Louise "Scout" Finch; Phillip Alford as Jem Finch; Brock Peters as Tom Robinson; Robert Duvall in his screen debut as Boo Radley
Directed by: Robert Mulligan

Cautions

Several intense moments involve children in peril. The court case at the center of the story is a rape trial. Though descriptive language is extremely discreet (accusations are usually rendered "he took advantage of me"), parents should be prepared for related discussion. Although negative racial slurs are occasionally used by bigots, their use is clearly condemned. Teens and adults should have no trouble navigating these issues.

Story Summary

A small-town lawyer in Depression-era Alabama confronts racism head-on when he defends a black man falsely accused of raping a white woman. Based on the Pulitzer Prize-winning novel by Harper Lee, *To Kill a Mockingbird* introduces one of the most honorable characters ever translated to the screen in Atticus Finch, a soft-spoken man of virtue whose wisdom, compassion, and integrity are matched only by his fatherly love. Gregory Peck won an Oscar for his portrayal of the gentle widower, a pillar of strength and intelligence who is as warm and inviting as a comfortable old chair when he patiently talks through his children's questions and worries ("There just didn't seem to be anyone or anything Atticus couldn't explain").

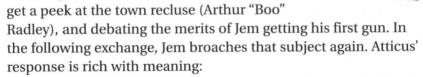

Even so, young Jem (10) and his tomboy sister, Scout (6), don't yet fully appreciate their father or the depth of his character. It's the summer of '32. The children are far too busy focusing on childish things, such as playing with their new neighbor (Dill Harris), trying to get a peek at the town recluse (Arthur "Boo" Radley), and debating the merits of Jem getting his first gun. In the following exchange, Jem broaches that subject again. Atticus' response is rich with meaning:

Jem: How old were you when you got your first gun, Atticus?

Atticus: Thirteen or fourteen. I remember when my daddy gave me that gun. He told me that I should never point at anything in the house and that he'd rather I shoot at tin cans in the backyard. But he said that sooner or later, he supposed, the temptation to go after birds would be too much, and that I could shoot all the blue jays I wanted—if I could hit 'em—but to remember 'twas a sin to kill a mockingbird.

Jem: Why?

Atticus: Well, I reckon because mockingbirds don't do anything but make music for us to enjoy. Don't eat people's gardens. Don't nest in the corncribs. They don't do one thing but just sing their hearts out for us.

Soon the children—and a community adorned in propriety but infected with prejudice—will realize what an extraordinary man Atticus really is. It's been 70 years since Abraham Lincoln freed the slaves, but in Maycomb, life hasn't changed much. Segregation reigns. So when a Negro named Tom Robinson is accused of raping Mayella Ewell, the daughter of a hard-drinking bigot, everyone expects it to be an open-and-shut case. Tom stands little chance of getting a fair trial. But no one figures on Atticus—tenacious in the pursuit of justice—being assigned as defense council. Over the course of a year, Atticus weathers cold shoulders, angry mobs, and other persecution as he fights to prove Tom's innocence. Meanwhile, Jem and Scout must also bear the weight of his convictions.

The trial itself is riveting. Despite compelling evidence that Mayella's father was actually the one who beat her up and that Tom is being made to take the fall, the jury turns its back on the facts. They find Tom guilty, though Atticus promises his client that he will wage an appeal. In a heartbreaking turn of events, Tom is reportedly shot and killed trying to escape. But the conflict isn't over for the Finch family. In a drunken rage, Bob Ewell stalks the children as they walk home from a school pageant. Jem is seriously hurt before a mysterious stranger intercedes and kills Ewell. It's Boo Radley. And a new friendship is formed.

Some teens may balk at black-and-white movies, but that visual style actually enhances the film's raw energy while capturing a sense of the time period. As the tale unfolds (viewed through the innocent eyes of a young girl) and builds to its climax, first-class performances and Horton Foote's brilliant screenplay will have everyone emotionally invested in the fate of good people battling social evil.

Before You Watch

Visit your local library or go online for information about the Great Depression. Understanding the economic climate of this simpler yet trying time in American history will give teens a better grasp of the story's context. One worthwhile resource is Robert S. McElvaine's book *The Great Depression: America, 1929-1941.*

Research race relations in the South circa 1930, specifically the real-life case involving nine young black men arrested in Scottsboro, Alabama, in 1931 for "raping" two white women (this event served as the basis for the Oscar-nominated documentary from 2000, *Scottsboro: An American Tragedy*). Teens who associate the end of slavery with the end of the Civil War may not realize how stratified the South stayed for decades after the Emancipation Proclamation.

Bible Bookmarks

Mk. 12:14; Tit. 2:7-8; Prov. 11:1-3; Eph. 4:29; Gen. 1:27; 1 Sam. 16:7; Jn. 8:31-32, 14:6, 17:17

Talking Points

1. What makes Atticus a good father? Why do Scout and Jem think he's pretty boring, and what do they learn about him during the course of the story?

2. What is integrity? Read Mark 12:14, Titus 2:7-8, and Proverbs 11:1-3. How do these verses contribute to your definition? Who in the story exhibits integrity and how? Talk about how Sheriff Tate decided to handle Bob Ewell's death. Was that the right thing to do? Why or why not?

3. How does the mockingbird conversation reprinted in the story summary apply to Tom Robinson? To Boo Radley?

4. More than once, Jem thinks he knows better than Atticus and disobeys him. What are the outcomes of these situations? Do you think Jem is justified in his defiance? Why or why not?

5. Both the book and the movie use racial slurs to degrade African Americans. For this and other reasons, *To Kill a Mockingbird* has been accused of promoting racism. What do you think? With which characters are we made to empathize, the ones who use that word or the ones who don't? What does Ephesians 4:29 have to say about the way we speak? (See Appendix I, "Language" section for further discussion.)

6. What does treating others with dignity entail? How does Atticus model this with the Cunninghams, Miss Dubose, Calpurnia, and others? Discuss his statement to Scout, "You never really understand a person until you consider things from his point of view . . . 'til you climb inside of his skin and walk around in it." Read Genesis 1:27. If all people are created in the image of God, how should we treat them? Ask your teen, "Is there anyone in your life whose skin you need to climb into right now?"

7. What does Scout's interaction with Mr. Cunningham outside the jail teach us about dealing with a "mob mentality"? Why is it sometimes easier for people to act up as part of a faceless group than as an individual?

8. Talk about stereotypes and superstitions. Both involve judging people based on superficial evidence or even rumors. Who in the film is a victim of stereotyping? What does the Bible say about this in 1 Samuel 16:7?

9. After Atticus presents his case, do you think the truth is clear to the jury? Why do they declare Tom Robinson guilty? Does our society always accept truth? Give some examples in which it does not. Read John 8:31-32, 14:6, and 17:17. In what ways might you be called upon to take an unpopular stand for truth?

10. Offer your teen a parent's perspective on Atticus' statement, "There's a lot of ugly things in this world, son. I wish I could keep 'em all away from you. That's never possible."

Follow-Up Activity

If he or she hasn't already done so, your teen will likely encounter the 1960 novel in high school English class. Why not take the initiative and go through it together? It's a fairly easy read that moves at a good pace. Reading *and* watching the same story can prompt comparison discussions. What were your favorite moments from the book? Were they included in the movie? If you'd been translating it to the screen, what might you have done differently?

Just for Fun

If you visit California and take the Universal Studios tour, you'll see the courthouse used in *To Kill a Mockingbird*. Of course, that's not the film most people would associate with this particular set. That same backlot building housed the famous clock tower in *Back to the Future*.

—*Lindy Beam*

The Truman Show

Rated: PG
Themes: Media exploitation, the search for truth, the power of fear and guilt, manipulation by a deceiver, voyeurism, caged safety vs. the dangers of freedom
Running Time: 1 hour, 43 Minutes
Starring: Jim Carrey as Truman Burbank; Ed Harris as Christof; Laura Linney as Meryl; Noah Emmerich as Marlon; Natascha McElhone as Sylvia
Directed by: Peter Weir

Cautions

About a dozen profanities, including several misuses of the Lord's name. Marlon frequently offers Truman beer.

Story Summary

"We've become bored with watching actors give us phony emotions. We're tired of pyrotechnics and special effects. While the world he inhabits is in some respects counterfeit, there's nothing fake about Truman himself. No scripts. No cue cards. It isn't always Shakespeare, but it's genuine. It's a life." —Christof

That life belongs to Truman Burbank, a naïve insurance salesman unaware that his hometown of Seahaven Island is actually an enormous television soundstage, and that 5,000 hidden cameras have been broadcasting his every move, 24/7, to the world for his entire life. Nearly 2 billion people witnessed his birth live via satellite. Truman's friends and family are actors. The significant events of his life have been orchestrated for dramatic effect. His closed-off community is a convincing collection of sets and props. And the ratings for this show, of which he knows nothing about, are *huge*.

Christof, the producer/director of this global reality show, is equal parts artist, sociologist, and entrepreneur. At one point Christof refers to himself as "the creator," [slight pause] ". . . of a television show," briefly hinting at his own megalomania. His God-like task is singular, if complex. He must continue a 30-year ruse, manipulating Truman's surroundings to make him believe in this created reality.

As the story unfolds, odd occurrences in the production cause Truman to suspect that something weird is going on. A rainstorm is somehow isolated over his head. At another point, he finds a radio station describing his every move. Bizarre obstacles keep him from leaving town. In one of the film's most powerful and unsettling scenes, Truman sits beside his lifelong friend Marlon and describes his frustration and confusion. "It feels like the whole world revolves around me somehow," Truman explains. "Everybody seems to be in on it!" With an understanding look and affirming tone, Marlon reminds Truman of how close they've been over the years, assuring him that there is no "it" to be in on. While the two talk, we discover that Christof is feeding Marlon every line through a tiny receiver in his ear. A chilling moment finds Marlon repeating Christof's cue, "I would gladly step in front of traffic for you Truman. And the last thing I would ever do is lie to you."

Later, during a Larry King-style interview, Christof is confronted by a caller angry over the prison-like life Truman has been forced to lead. Chistof's reply is telling. "He can leave at any time," he says. "If his was more than just a vague ambition, if he was absolutely determined to discover the truth, there's no way we could prevent him. I think what distresses you . . . is that ultimately, Truman prefers his 'cell', as you call it."

After unraveling the deception, Truman summons that absolute determination, confounding the watchful eye of Big Brother and making his move. A manhunt ensues. Truman overcomes his lifelong anxiety about water and sets sail—literally—on a search for truth. In the master control room, Christof activates a violent storm. Truman refuses to turn back. After Christof causes his boat to capsize, Truman manages to survive and reach the outer edge of his counterfeit world. The voice of Christof bellows forth, desperately trying to convince Truman to stay. He warns of the dangers on the outside, suggesting that it's safer where he is. Even so, Truman leaves this "cell" to boldly take his chances with whatever may exist in the unpredictable, *real* world.

Before You Watch

Use dinnertime conversation to ask teens what they see as obstacles that keep people from accepting the truth. Examples might include the following:

- *Ignorance* (They've never heard it)
- *Apathy* (They don't care about it)
- *Rebellion* (They're too proud to listen)
- *Fear* (That newfound knowledge will demand something of them)

Bible Bookmarks

Matt. 5:11-12; Jn. 8:31-32, 44; Mk. 4:13-20; 1 Cor. 4:11-13; 2 Cor. 2:11, 10:5, 11:14; Lk. 4:1-13, 18:17; Eph. 6:10-17; 1 Pet. 5:8

Talking Points

1. How is Christof similar to Satan as the master of deception exposed in John 8:44, and in 2 Corinthians 2:11 and 11:14? Consider this statement: "If you are tempted, you know it. If you are oppressed or abused, you know it. But if you are deceived, you don't know it." Satan's lies can only be countered by seeking and embracing truth as God has revealed it in the Bible (Luke 4:1-13). Be sure to identify ways we're told to arm ourselves for spiritual warfare (1 Peter 5:8, Ephesians 6:10-17).

2. We often sense a reality beyond what we see and experience, but must overcome the obstacles of complacency and deception Satan throws our way. How is Truman like individuals described in the parable of the sower (Mark 4:13-20)? Read Jesus' words in John 8:31-32 and

talk about how Truman's experience is similar to mankind's search for truth.

3. Christof says Truman could discover the truth if he were "absolutely determined" to do so. Can a person discover the spiritual truth of the gospel without being deeply determined? What does the Bible say is required (read Luke 18:17)? What "cells" hinder people's progress?

4. Christof cautions Truman against leaving the safety of deception for the dangers of reality. With the help of verses such as Matthew 5:11-12 and 1 Corinthians 4:11-13, discuss how encountering and living in truth can be more difficult and dangerous than living a lie.

5. Is Truman's obsession with finding Sylvia appropriate? Since it seems to be the most genuine relationship he's ever had, it's easy to root for them to reunite. But until Meryl leaves him, Truman is (as far as he knows) a legitimately married man. Talk about that moral conundrum.

6. How did the producers prey on Truman's fears, and how did that keep him from becoming anything more than what they had planned for him? Consider the subtle messages crafted to undermine Truman's self-confidence. Discuss the ability of the media to manipulate people's emotions and why Christians must follow the words of 2 Corinthians 10:5.

7. Who is ultimately to blame for Truman's years of bondage? Christof? The actors? The sponsors? Or is it the multitude of viewers riveted to their TV screens? Explore the culpability of each.

8. Look closely at Christof's statement at the beginning of the story summary. How is his opinion of the public's appetite for entertainment reflected in reality TV shows like *Survivor* or MTV's *The Real World*?

9. When *The Truman Show* was first released, director Peter Weir said, "I think there's a kind of image virus. Images are so manipulated now. You can't be sure what you're looking at. Is it a re-creation? Is it actual? Is it fiction? Does it matter? Children see violence on TV so much that they don't know what's real or unreal." Would you agree or disagree with his statement? Why?

10. Ask teens what they make of the security guards' responses to the end of "The Truman Show" in the film's final scene. Then ask what they think about the countless viewers like them who passively observed Truman's life at the expense of their own adventures. If necessary, suggest some things both Truman and the show's viewers could have missed out on (truth, suffering, love, reality, etc.).

11. Some young viewers might equate Christof with a controlling parent afraid to let go of an adolescent wanting to explore a dangerous,

cruel world. Take a moment to talk about Christof and Truman's relationship from that perspective.

Follow-Up Activity

Consider visiting a local music or video store. Some artists and producers overtly and unapologetically promote immoral or satanic messages and themes. Look at CD covers, song titles, movie and computer game themes, magazine covers, etc. Identify several that promote themes or send messages that are part of our enemy's "grand deception." Examples can be as obvious as attacks on God or as subtle as suggesting that sex outside of marriage is fun and harmless.

Just for Fun

In the role of Christof, Ed Harris won a Golden Globe and was nominated for an Oscar in the Best Supporting Actor category.

His acceptance speech should have included a great big "thank you" to fellow thespian Dennis Hopper. It seems Hopper was originally cast as Christof, but walked off the set after only one day on the job. His loss proved to be Harris' gain.

—*Kurt Bruner*

Unbreakable

Rated: PG-13
Themes: Good vs. evil, personal sacrifice, the father/son bond, justice, heroism, working through marital trials, fulfilling one's calling
Running Time: 1 hour, 47 minutes
Starring: Bruce Willis as David Dunne; Samuel L. Jackson as Elijah Price; Robin Wright Penn as Audrey Dunne; Spencer Treat Clark as Joseph Dunne
Directed by: M. Night Shyamalan

Cautions

This psychological thriller is *not* for everyone. Some viewers will find the film's somber tone oppressive and the scene involving a terrorized family disturbing. For fans of suspense, however, it's one of the most restrained and redemptive entries the genre has seen in a long time. Moments of intense conflict (more implied than explicit) involve a violent train wreck, physical assaults, and bodies found murdered. A boy pulls a gun on his father, but doesn't shoot. In a discreetly handled snapshot premonition, a man considers taking advantage of a girl who has passed out. There are a mere seven profanities, though several are misuses of the Lord's name (you can avoid three of them, as well as a crude crack about masturbation, without losing any key story points by simply muting or fast-forwarding through the two minutes or so of Elijah in the city comic store).

Story Summary

It's 1961 and a baby boy has just been born in a Philadelphia department store. A doctor announces that his arms and legs were broken during labor . . .

We then arrive in the present-day, where security guard David Dunne sits on a commuter train, heading home after a job interview. The train crashes. David is the sole survivor. Somehow he has escaped without a scratch and is met at the hospital by his estranged wife, Audrey, and adoring 12-year-old son, Joseph.

Soon after, David finds a mysterious card on his windshield which reads, *How many days of your life have you been sick?* He can't recall a single one. Neither can Audrey. When David's boss of five years confirms that he has never taken a sick day, David follows the address on the card to Elijah Price, the frail-boned comic book art dealer whose birth we witnessed earlier. As a boy, Elijah was called Mr. Glass by his schoolmates. He breaks easily. Only after his mother began bribing him out of his solitude with comic books did he venture outside. Now this intelligent yet deeply embittered man is convinced luck had nothing to do with David's survival, but that he's an unbreakable, postmodern superhero with a noble destiny. No one

wants to believe this more than Joseph, who already idolizes his dad. However, David thinks Elijah is a nut and returns to his sad daily existence, which gets a nice shot in the arm when Audrey—equally sure that her husband's survival was no fluke—decides they should make the most of this second chance and work through their marital problems.

Elijah appears at the stadium where David works and suggests that maybe David chose to be a security guard because of his desire to protect people. David gets a premonition about a gun tucked into a man's belt. The suspicious man escapes down a flight of stairs. Elijah tries to follow and falls, shattering his glass cane and many bones. But as the man hurdles a turnstile, Elijah gets his proof.

David continues to deny that he's anything special, but Joseph wants to prove otherwise and even threatens to shoot his father, positive that he will walk away unscathed. After a tense standoff, the parents decide this game has gone far enough, though several events happen that cause David to wonder if Elijah might actually be onto something.

Elijah tells David to visit a crowded place to test his gift. In a busy train station, he brushes against people and gets flashes of the evil deeds they'll soon commit. One commands David's attention and leads him to a house where he finds a man and woman murdered, and two young girls bound. (This scene may disturb some viewers, but like all of the conflict in *Unbreakable,* it is intense but not excessively graphic.) David battles with the killer, eventually breaking the brute's neck.

Having discovered his "calling," David has a new lease on life. He has witnessed healing in his marriage. He feels worthy of his son's adoration. When he goes to the art gallery to thank Elijah, he shakes his hand and is shocked by the vision he receives. It seems every superhero must have a nemesis, and David is sickened to have finally unmasked his.

Before You Watch

While watching the evening news together, discuss the apparent dominance of evil in this world. Revelation 19:11-21 tells us that good will ultimately triumph. Why, then, does evil seem so much more powerful here on earth? Read Matthew 12:35 and 1 John 5:19.

Bible Bookmarks

Gen. 3:1; Matt. 4:5-7, 12:35, 28:16-20; 1 Jn. 5:19; Rev. 19:11-21; Ps. 94; Rom. 8:28; 1 Thes. 5:14-15; Jn. 8:44; Lk. 10:25-37; 2 Cor. 2:11, 11:14

Talking Points

1. This film taps into the underlying passion all humans have for a supernatural hero. We are created to long for that personality who is looking out for us, has a virtuous heart, and has the unique ability to answer our cries for help. A superhero. A savior. A messiah. Read Psalm 94 and discuss how *Unbreakable* draws upon the divine drama as explained in Appendix II.

2. Elijah's mother tells her withdrawn preteen son, "You might fall

between this chair and that television. If that's what God has planned for you, that's what's gonna happen." Talk about her theology. Romans 8:28 says the Lord can make all things work for good, but is every stumble in life "predetermined" by God?

3. How did you feel toward Elijah at the end of the movie? Did you pity him for being physically disabled and mentally challenged, or did his horrible acts of terrorism make it impossible for you to sympathize with his anguish? Is it possible to despise his behavior and turn him in (as David did), *and* show compassion for a person's condition?

4. Talk about Joseph's relationship with his father. Have you ever wanted so desperately to believe something that you were tempted to boldly put your faith to the test as Joseph did when he considered shooting David? What was it? How do Jesus' words in Matthew 4:5-7 warn Christians to be careful in this area?

5. Analyze the complex nature of David and Audrey's marital troubles, including their impact on Joseph. Although we don't know all of the details, what might they have done to avoid sliding to that place? It's rare to see a couple actually working through trials this way in a movie. Why do you think that is?

6. Joseph sticks up for weaker classmates, adhering to "the hero's code" ("You can't let bad things happen to good people"). How does this attitude reflect 1 Thessalonians 5:14-15? Was David justified in killing the evil intruder? Why or why not? How did that scene make you feel, specifically for David and for the victims?

7. David's decision to fake an injury and give up football for the sake of true love was quite a sacrifice. Talk about that. As a physical therapist Audrey contends, "Football in many ways is the opposite of what I do. You're rewarded the more you punish your opponent. It's too much about violence." What do you think of her perspective?

8. What do you think was the source of David's sadness? How much will things change now that he has found his purpose in life? Do you agree with Elijah's assertion that the scariest thing is "to not know your place in this world—to not know why you're here"? As Christians, how is our purpose made plain in Scripture (Matthew 28:16-20, Luke 10:25-37)? Have you felt a deep conviction about what you want to do with your life? Have you talked to God about it? What has He shown you?

9. After reading Luke 10:25-37, ask teens to imagine what it would be like to be a full-time "Good Samaritan."

10. There are two kinds of villains described by Elijah's mother in the closing scene; the "soldier villain who fights the hero with his hands" and the "brilliant and evil archenemy who fights the hero with his mind." Which more closely resembles our spiritual nemesis, Satan? Why? Read Genesis 3:1, John 8:44, and 2 Corinthians 2:11 and 11:14.

 ## Follow-Up Activity

Visit a comic book store together and examine some popular titles. Discuss typical rules comic books follow (super powers, secret identities, weaknesses such as Kryptonite, and so on) and ask your teen, "What themes do you see in these tales that are also found in some Bible stories?"

Just for Fun

In a scene at the stadium, David stops a man he thinks may be carrying drugs. The dark-haired suspect is none other than *Unbreakable*'s writer/director/producer, M. Night Shyamalan.

—*Mick Silva*

Appendix I: Hollywood and the Bible

While dissecting motion pictures can lead to all sorts of teachable moments, some families have their most stimulating discussions across the dinner table or during long drives. Here we've compiled some jumping-off points for those occasions when you want to spark a lively conversation on the subject of Hollywood, the Bible, or just when you want to follow up on a particular subject.

Character

"Finally, brothers, whatever is true, whatever is noble, whatever is right, whatever is pure, whatever is lovely, whatever is admirable—if anything is excellent or praiseworthy—think about such things" (Philippians 4:8). *Positive films endow their heroes with nobility. Others might portray the hero as being above God's moral standard. Either way, the fruits of the Spirit (Galatians 5:22-23) are the character qualities to shoot for.*

"Do not envy wicked men, do not desire their company; for their hearts plot violence, and their lips talk about making trouble" (Proverbs 24:1-2). *Bad company corrupts good character (1 Corinthians 15:33), whether that companionship is sought in human friendships or felt as part of a kinship with figures onscreen.*

Despair

"Today, many of Hollywood's most successful films argue that happiness is an illusion, striving is futile and values are a myth. . . . When Hollywood continually tells impressionable adolescents that life is a hopeless, meaningless trap, is it so surprising that some choose to exit in a blaze of Wagnerian glory?" —Columnist Don Feder on how the media sets the stage for real-life teen murders and suicides[1]

Discernment

"I've always felt that, as an entertainer, my job is to tell a story and make people feel things, which may not always mean taking the moral high ground. If a teenager can't discern right from wrong . . . I'm pretty confident that it has little to do with whether he or she watches *Buffy* or plays aggressive video games, and more to do with the fact that society has failed to teach him or her how to make those distinctions." —Actress Sarah Michelle Gellar *(Cruel Intentions, I Know What You Did Last Summer,* TV's *Buffy the Vampire Slayer)*[2]

Human Nature
"The heart is deceitful above all things and beyond cure. Who can understand it?" (Jeremiah 17:9). *A lot of films—romances in particular—laud living for the moment and following one's heart. But following the whims of the heart without evaluating those desires based on God's Word can open the door to self-deception and lead to trouble.*

Language
"Civilization is a bootstrap operation. We have to make a point of being civilized. . . . Dirty words in a movie make everyone in the audience less civil by reducing them to what they're forced to think by what they hear together." —An Oscar-night social commentary by *60 Minutes* curmudgeon Andy Rooney[3]

"Put away perversity from your mouth; keep corrupt talk far from your lips" (Proverbs 4:24). *One of the ways we can avoid using profanity and other forms of "corrupt talk" is to avoid getting used to* hearing *it in entertainment. That includes coarse joking (Ephesians 5:4) and misuses of the Lord's name (Exodus 20:7).*

Perspective
"Rejoice with those who rejoice; mourn with those who mourn" (Romans 12:15). *Empathy is more than a virtue; it's a spiritual command. One of the ways parents can help teens develop greater empathy is by encouraging them to view onscreen circumstances through the eyes of various characters. Usually the audience is conditioned to see events from only the hero's perspective.*

"[Movie characters'] ideals become our ideals. Their thoughts become standards of our thinking and language. Their style of dress and movement are seen on the streets of our nation. And their moments of triumph and defeat become our successes and our failures." —Actress Jodi Foster *(Silence of the Lambs, Panic Room)* speaking on behalf of the American Film Institute concerning the power of motion pictures to shape the culture[4]

Preserving Innocence

"You cannot experience the thrill of a first kiss when you've heard and seen everything long before you're ready. If the counterrevolution against the sexual revolution is to be won, it will not be fear of AIDS or pregnancy that will tip the balance. It will be a longing for the excitement, the mystery and the sweetness, which has youthful innocence as its prerequisite." —Syndicated columnist Mona Charen describing the price children pay for growing up too fast[5]

"I will set before my eyes no vile thing. The deeds of faithless men I hate; they will not cling to me" (Psalm 101:3). *What we see on-screen can stoke lust in our hearts (2 Sam. 11:2, 1 Jn. 2:16). Therefore, we should do our best to avoid consuming and filing away unhealthy visuals. As for the second part of this verse, the deeds of faithless men and women are frequently paraded across the screen as something heroic today. Help teens see them for what they really are.*

"Flee from sexual immorality. All other sins a man commits are outside his body, but he who sins sexually sins against his own body. Do you not know that your body is a temple of the Holy Spirit, who is in you, whom you have received from God? You are not your own; you were bought at a price. Therefore honor God with your body" (1 Corinthians 6:18-20). *Since Jesus equated a lustful thought life with physical infidelity (Matthew 5:27-29), movies that prey on people's sin nature at either level should be out of bounds.*

Responsibility

"The great thing about film is it's a true democracy. People vote with their dollars. And as long as they keep paying to see it, then we get to keep making movies." —Writer/producer Dean Devlin *(Independence Day, Godzilla, The Patriot)*[6]

"I tell you that men will have to give account on the day of judgment for every careless word they have spoken" (Matthew 12:36). *Even though films are scripted (some more meticulously than others), they're often filled with careless comments, language, and ideology that grieves the heart of God.*

"Television people have put blinders on, and they absolutely refuse— and movie people too—to admit that they can have any influence for ill in our society. You know the argument: 'We only reflect what's going on; we don't perpetuate it.' And yet not a week goes by in this town where there's not an award ceremony where they're patting each other on the back saying, 'You raised AIDS awareness' [or] 'There'll be no more child abuse thanks to that fine show you did.' The argument is you can only influence for good; you can't influence for ill. That makes no sense at all." —*Wheel of Fortune* host Pat Sajak addressing Hollywood's double-standard[7]

"Movies both reflect and create social conditions, but their special charm is to offer a world where people consume without the tedium of labor. Characters float in a world where the bill never comes due . . . and we wonder why we're a debtor nation." —Molly Haskell from the book *Consuming Desires*[8]

Violence

"The LORD examines the righteous, but the wicked and those who love violence his soul hates" (Psalm 11:5). *There's a difference between violent conflict that is historical or incidental, and the kind of brutality that is packaged as its own visceral reward. From slasher films with a high body count to R-rated actioners, Hollywood often caters to lovers of violence.*

World View

"Just as man is destined to die once, and after that to face judgment . . ." (Hebrews 9:27). *Whether part of a supernatural thriller, a sci-fi epic, or the biography of Gandhi, reincarnation and pantheism are popular in Tinseltown, which has a soft spot for Eastern thought.*

Appendix II: The Power of Story

Why use stories to teach moral concepts? The authors of *The Family New Media Guide* note: "It's vital that youngsters learn the rules of good behavior, but exhortations about responsibility seem to fall on deaf ears, and discussions of abstract concepts such as justice fail to hold their attention. . . . Stories work where abstract principles do not because stories take advantage of our natural need to make a narrative of our own lives. It's one of the ways we have of making sense of sacrifices we make and sufferings we endure. Without the conviction that our life constitutes a meaningful story, it makes little sense to deny ourselves immediate gratifications, little sense to look beyond the pleasures of the moment."[1]

While teaching a class at a Christian writer's conference, I asked how many had watched the movie *It's a Wonderful Life*. Out of nearly 100 students, all but two raised their hands. "And how many of you have watched that movie more than once?" The same people again raised their hands.

Why do we return to a story we've seen or read many times? We know all the plot twists and how the drama will end. Understanding what's behind your return to a favorite book or movie can add a new dimension to the viewing of films with your teenage son or daughter. That's what this section is about—*what makes a great story*.

My friend Kurt Bruner has said:

"We love *Romeo and Juliet* because it is a passionate romance.

"We love Indiana Jones because it is a grand adventure.

"We love Sherlock Holmes because it is an unsolved mystery.

"We love *The Hunchback of Notre Dame* because it is a touching tragedy.

"We love *The Lord of the Rings* because it is a heroic quest.

"We love *Rocky* because a nice underdog wins.

"We love *Star Wars* because the evil villain loses.

"And we love the gospel because it is all of the above!"

Whether the storyteller, film director, or movie producer knows it or not, all great stories at their heart reflect the greatest story, the grand drama of the gospel. That is the true story that all others are trying to

169

tell. Let's take the popular Christmas film *It's a Wonderful Life* and examine the structural elements that make it work. The same structural elements operate within every good story, including the gospel.

An effective story begins with a protagonist that we care about.
The protagonist is the central character in the story. George Bailey, played by Jimmy Stewart, is the protagonist in *It's a Wonderful Life*. Of course, there are other important characters as well. Most good stories have subplots, each with its own protagonist. Two subplots in this movie involve Clarence, the angel, and Mary, George's wife. But let's concentrate on the primary protagonist. A good story is built around one character who:

- has a strong need or desire (and knows it)
- may also have an unconscious desire
- has the will and opportunity to pursue that desire
- has at least a chance to satisfy the desire.

In their simplest terms, a boy wants to win a girl's heart in a romance. In an adventure, the protagonist wants to climb the mountain or find the treasure. In a mystery, the detective wants to find out who committed the murder. George Bailey wants something. He wants to get out of the miserable little town of Bedford Falls and see the world. He wants to do great things with his life. His plan is to leave home, go to college, then see the world. And for a time, it appears he will get his wish. However, George also has an unconscious desire, something that only emerges later in the drama: The thing he's *really* looking for is meaning and significance in his life. Of course, a good story doesn't allow the protagonist to proceed unimpeded toward his goal. Therefore . . .

An effective story needs a powerful force of antagonism.
A story is only as compelling as the strength of the forces of antagonism that provide obstacles to the protagonist's object of desire. Further, the success of the protagonist is only as satisfying as the degree of antagonism he overcomes.

We celebrate David's victory over Goliath because Goliath was an unbeatable giant. In *Hoosiers,* we root for the small-town basketball team to beat the school many times its size in the championship. In *Ever After,* we cheer when the peasant girl wins the heart of the prince. The greater the odds, the bigger the victory!

The force of antagonism doesn't have to be human. At first, we might think that George Bailey's antagonist is Mr. Potter, who owns all of the town except the building and loan, which is run by George. In some respects, Mr. Potter is the antagonist. But as we'll see, he's not the ultimate force of antagonism in this story, and that's one of the reasons why this movie is so timeless.

What prevents George Bailey from pursuing his dream? First of all, it is the circumstances of life. He needs the money to go away. When he finally gets it, on the night before he is leaving for college, his father has a stroke and dies. George needs to stay and take care of his father's affairs. He fulfills his obligations and is ready to leave when he learns that the building and loan, his father's legacy, will be shut down by Potter unless he takes over. Again and again, George is blocked from achieving his dream. But the strength of this timeless story is that the most powerful force of antagonism lies within George, not in his circumstances or in the person of Mr. Potter. More on that in a minute.

As with the protagonist, there is a force of antagonism for each subplot as well. The next time you watch *It's a Wonderful Life*, see if you can identify the forces of antagonism for the angel Clarence and for Mary Bailey. With the protagonist and forces of antagonism in place, we are now ready to observe the six elements of story.

1. Ordinary World
The ordinary world is the protagonist's world at peace. It may or may not be the world as he likes it. It's just the way it is. In some stories, this ordinary world is implied. For other stories, it may take up to 20 or 25 percent of the story to establish enough about a protagonist's world to make the drama meaningful.

The ordinary world of George Bailey is provided through glances shown to the angel Clarence. George is a local hero—he saved his brother from drowning as a boy. He prevented the pharmacist from making a tragic mistake. He is popular with the girls. He has a bad ear. But most important, George is looking beyond Bedford Falls. He has a dream to see the world and make his fortune.

2. Creation of Imbalance
The creation of imbalance is the event that shifts the protagonist out of his ordinary world and into a quest on which he must either succeed or at least regain balance in his life. It is usually a single event that happens to the protagonist, directly impacts the protagonist, or is caused by the protagonist.

For George Bailey, the pivotal defining event in his life is the death of his father. Suddenly, his world turns upside down. He can't—in good conscience—leave town. He must take responsibility for his father's affairs and business. But of course, George's dream hasn't died.

3. Active Pursuit of Desire
A great story consists of a series of events of increasing intensity in which the protagonist pursues his desire. It begins with the first, easiest step. For George, that means taking care of his father's estate so he can then continue on with his plans to go to college. But the board of the building and loan decides to close the business unless George stays on as director. Over time, it appears George is helping others achieve their dreams, but he is trapped—he cannot leave Bedford Falls.

4. Progressive Antagonism
At each step, as the protagonist pursues his goal, he must be faced with forces of antagonism, and each confrontation must raise the stakes to a higher level. In *Fiddler on the Roof,* a great example involves Tevye's daughters' intensified breaking of tradition. In *It's a Wonderful Life,* Potter represents the force of antagonism to George, at first by belittling him and his father and the "insignificant" building and loan. Later, Potter increases the pressure on George by seizing an opportunity to steal a large deposit.

But what makes this story special is a twist in the middle of the film when Potter presents George with the answer to his dreams. Potter offers George a three-year contract at $20,000 per year, a huge amount for the time, with a chance to travel to New York and overseas. Here George has what he wants dropped into his lap. But, of course, at a price: He must let the building and loan die, and that means the people he's been helping will no longer have an advocate. He may not understand it yet, but George realizes that there is something more important in life than his own personal happiness.

5. Ultimate Confrontation and Climax
The protagonist and the ultimate force of antagonism must face off in a final confrontation. This is the point in the story when the stakes cannot get any higher. The protagonist must achieve his goal or "die" trying. However, the ultimate confrontation is not always the one you expect. Here it is precipitated by Potter's theft of an $8,000 deposit just as the

bank examiner is about to look at the building and loan's books. In desperation, George pleads with Potter for a loan.

George: You're the only one in town that can help me.

Potter: What kind of security would I have, George? Have you got any stocks?

George: No, sir.

Potter: Bonds? Real estate? Collateral of any kind?

George: I have some life insurance, a fifteen thousand dollar policy.

Potter: How much is your equity in it?

George: Five hundred dollars.

Potter: (sneering) You're worth more dead than alive.

That's what precipitates the ultimate conflict. George decides the only way to solve his problems is to commit suicide. As far as he can tell, he hasn't achieved any of the desires he had in life. In fact, he tells his guardian angel, "I wish I'd never been born." Clarence, as we all know, grants him that wish. George Bailey is allowed to see his family, his loved ones, and the town of Bedford Falls as they would have been had he never lived. And that's what causes George to discover what he really wants in life.

6. Resolution

It's interesting that nothing has changed about George Bailey's life after the climax. He's still trapped in Bedford Falls. As far as he knows, $8,000 is still missing. He's sure he's going to jail. And yet everything has changed, because George realizes that what he wants in life is significance and meaning. He now likes the fact that his brother is a war hero because George saved him as a boy. He appreciates all the families that own their homes because he found a way to give them loans. And he desperately wants to see his wife and children, for he can't imagine how he can live without them.

Naturally, we want the happy ending. We want the problems resolved. And of course, they are. Mary has spread the word about the crisis, and all the people George has helped over the years come to his aid. People pour into the house and give generously—more than what's needed to replace the stolen cash. And so, life is restored to a new "ordinary world" for George Bailey. New because George is a changed man. He's no longer looking beyond Bedford Falls for adventure and significance, for he has found it at home with his family and community.

Consciously or unconsciously we enjoy a movie like *It's a Wonderful*

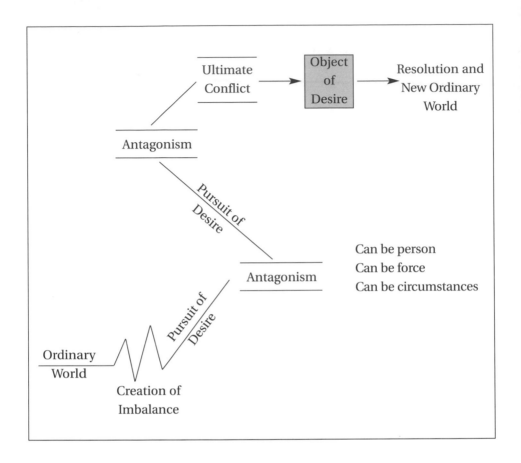

Life because it presents a facet of the Grand Drama that is the gospel story. George Bailey represents the yearning for meaning and significance in our less-than-satisfying circumstances. Each of us must somehow answer the questions, "Who am I?" and "Why am I here?" We love this film because at the deepest level, in our souls, we identify with George Bailey's journey. We don't know the end of our own story, but we're uplifted by the hope that we, like George, can discover that life is truly worth living.

What does this have to do with the gospel? We tend to look at presentations like *The Four Spiritual Laws* as the gospel message. In fact, they are actually the punch line to a grand drama in which God is the protagonist. That story, the greatest story ever told, follows the same structure as we've just observed in *It's a Wonderful Life*. There are many ways to tell the story. Let's look at just one that we might call "The Great Romance."

Ordinary World: Once upon a time, God lived in glorious splendor in heaven among His angels. At one point, before *our* story begins, there was a revolt and God's most glorious angel, Lucifer, was cast out of heaven along with about one third of the angels. However, that event did nothing to disturb the perfect harmony that existed among the Father, Son, and Holy Spirit.

Creation of Imbalance: God decided He wanted a lover, a creature of His making who would choose to worship Him. God created His beloved, a man and a woman, and placed them in a beautiful garden. There, the three of them enjoyed sweet fellowship until that horrible day when God's sworn enemy seduced His beloved. Here God was, on His honeymoon, and His bride was unfaithful.

Active Pursuit of Desire: God set out to win back the heart of His beloved. It was an arduous process. First, He approached a single man, Abraham, and entered into a covenant with him and his descendents. As the children of Abraham grew, God expanded the terms of the covenant, providing detailed laws for the people to purify themselves so they could approach the most holy God. But His beloved often wandered away and worshipped other gods. Finally, to demonstrate His love, God sent His Son to earth, disguised in human form.

Progressive Antagonism: The victory of the protagonist is only as satisfying as the strength of the force of antagonism. Most people see Satan as the antagonist, and he certainly is. But God faced a far more formidable foe within Himself. For on the one hand, God loved His people and wanted to have a relationship with them. On the other hand, God's justice demanded that He punish His beloved for her unfaithfulness, and the punishment was death. If He were faithful to His justice, He would lose the object of His desire. How could God reconcile His love and His justice?

Ultimate Confrontation and Climax: God's love and justice met at the cross! The prophet Isaiah said, "It was the LORD's will to crush him and cause him to suffer" (Isaiah 53:10). God the father poured all the wrath that rightly should have been directed at us upon Jesus. God the Son, for the love of His people, accepted the horror of God's wrath and bore all of the punishment that should have been ours.

Resolution: The Resurrection! When Jesus conquered death we were permitted, through the Holy Spirit, to again enjoy the fellowship with God that the first couple knew in the Garden of Eden. However, each person still must choose: Will I accept the love offered or not?

That's God's story in a nutshell. Of course, there are so many rich turns and nuances that these few paragraphs really can't do it justice. Every great big-screen romance that puts a lump in our throats in some way reflects this great love story.

Of course, God's story can also be told as a great adventure of a king who loses his kingdom and has to go to war to win it back. Or it can be told as the story of a father whose children run away, and he must go on a journey to a far land to find them and bring them home. Adventure stories, mysteries, dramas—we love them because they reflect a greater reality. The structure of a story reveals these divine elements.

And so, when you watch the films dissected in this book, you might think about taking some time to analyze the structure. See if you can identify the ordinary world of the protagonist. What is the creation of imbalance? How does the protagonist pursue the object of his or her desire, and what is the force of antagonism that creates obstacles to reaching that goal? As you ask these questions, you may find that you also gain insights into the greatest story of all, the divine drama that gives meaning to our lives.

• • •

Note: For more information on the gospel story, I highly recommend *The Grand Drama* by Kurt Bruner, Tyndale House Publishers, 2001.

—*Al Janssen*

Notes

Introduction: Getting the Most out of Movie Nights

1. BBC TV Series, *Panorama*, "The Killing Screens," originally aired February 27, 1995.
2. From an interview with the actress in *Teen People*, August, 1999.
3. From an interview with the publisher in *Vibe*, September 2001.
4. Addressing students at Fisk University in Nashville, Tenn., April 9, 1996.
5. *Mind Over Media* video produced by Focus on the Family, 2000.
6. From statistics published in *Entertainment Weekly*, March 29, 2002.
7. From an article in *Newsweek*, December 11, 2000.
8. From an exposé about "stealth marketing" in movies in *Talk*, November, 2001.
9. Dudley Nichols, "The Writer and the Film," *Theatre Arts*, October 1943.
10. William Kilpatrick, Gregory Wolfe, and Suzanne M. Wolfe, *The Family New Media Guide* (New York: Touchstone, 1997), p. 37.
11. *USA Today*, May 14, 1999.
12. Kenneth A. Myers, *All God's Children and Blue Suede Shoes: Christians and Popular Culture* (Wheaton: Crossway Books, 1989).

Appendix I: Hollywood vs. the Bible

1. From an article in *Conservative Chronicle*, March 29, 2000.
2. From an article in *Cosmopolitan*, March 2000.
3. From CBS's program *60 Minutes*, originally aired March 25, 2001.
4. CBS program, "American Film Institute's 100 Years . . . 100 Movies," air date June 16, 1998.
5. From an article in *Conservative Chronicle*, January 5, 2000.
6. From an article in *Premiere*, June 1998.
7. PBS's *National Desk*, "The Popular Culture: Who's to Blame?" aired January 29, 1999.
8. Molly Haskell, originally quoted in the book *Consuming Desires* (Shearwater Books, 1999), reprinted in *Reader's Digest*, March 2000.

Appendix II: The Power of Story

1. William Kilpatrick, Gregory Wolfe, and Suzanne M. Wolfe, *The Family New Media Guide* (New York: Touchstone, 1997), pp. 26-27.

Additional information throughout the text courtesy of The Internet Movie Database, www.IMDb.com. Used with permission.

About the General Editor

Bob Smithouser is editor of *Plugged In* magazine, Focus on the Family's award-winning parents' guide to entertainment and popular youth culture. He is also the ministry's chief movie reviewer at *pluggedinmag.com*.

About the Writers

Kurt Bruner is a vice president at Focus on the Family, where he leads in the creation of books, films, magazines, and radio drama, including the popular Adventures in Odyssey series and the Peabody Award-winning Focus on the Family Radio Theatre programs.

Al Janssen has written or co-authored 26 books, including *The Marriage Masterpiece* (Focus on the Family). He is currently Writer-in-Residence for Open Doors with Brother Andrew.

Larry Weeden is the director of book development for Focus on the Family and has written or co-authored 20 books.

Lindy Beam is a resident supervisor at the Focus on the Family Institute. Prior to beginning her work with college students, she was a part of the *Plugged In* magazine team for three years.

Steven Isaac edits and manages *Plugged In Online*, serves as associate editor for *Plugged In* magazine and editor for *Plugged In*'s weekly "Culture Clips."

Lissa Halls Johnson is a book producer, writer, and fiction acquisitions editor for Focus on the Family. She is the creator and editor of the Brio Girls book series. She has written 15 novels for teenagers and young readers.

Shana Murph is an editor and writer in book publishing. She resides in Philadelphia, Pennsylvania.

Mick Silva is an associate editor in Focus on the Family's book publishing department.

Welcome to the Family!

Heritage Builders®

Helping You Build a Family of Faith

We hope you've enjoyed this book. Heritage Builders was founded in 1995 by three fathers with a passion for the next generation. As a ministry of Focus on the Family, Heritage Builders strives to equip, train, and motivate parents to become intentional about building a strong spiritual heritage.

It's quite a challenge for busy parents to find ways to build a spiritual foundation for their families—especially in a way they enjoy and understand. Through activities and participation, children can learn biblical truth in ways they can understand, enjoy—and *remember.*

Passing along a heritage of Christian faith to your family is a parent's highest calling. Heritage Builders' goal is to encourage and empower you in this great mission with practical resources and inspiring ideas that really work—and help your children develop a lasting love for God.

* * *

How To Reach Us

For more information, visit our Heritage Builders Web site! Log on to **www.heritagebuilders.com** to discover new resources, sample activities and ideas to help you pass on a spiritual heritage. To request any of these resources, simply call Focus on the Family at 1-800-A-FAMILY (1-800-232-6459) or in Canada, call 1-800-661-9800. Or send your request to Focus on the Family, Colorado Springs, CO 80995. In Canada, write Focus on the Family, P.O. Box 9800, Stn. Terminal, Vancouver, B.C. V6B 4G3

To learn more about Focus on the Family or to find out if there is an associate office in your country, please visit www.family.org

We'd love to hear from you!

Every family has a heritage—a spiritual, emotional, and social legacy passed from one generation to the next. There are four main areas we at Heritage Builders recommend parents consider as they plan to pass their faith to their children:

Family Fragrance

Every family's home has a fragrance. Heritage Builders encourages parents to create a home environment that fosters a sweet, Christ-centered "AROMA" of love through Affection, Respect, Order, Merriment, and Affirmation.

Family Traditions

Whether you pass down stories, beliefs, and/or customs, traditions can help you establish a special identity for your family. Heritage Builders encourages parents to set special "milestones" for their children to help guide them and move them through their spiritual development.

Family Compass

Parents have the unique task of setting standards for normal, healthy living through their attitudes, actions, and beliefs. Heritage Builders encourages parents to give their children the moral navigation tools they need to succeed on the road of life.

Family Moments

Creating special, teachable moments with their children is one of a parent's most precious and sometimes most difficult responsibilities. Heritage Builders encourages parents to capture little moments throughout the day to teach and impress values, beliefs, and biblical principles upon their children.

We look forward to standing alongside you as you seek to impart the Lord's care and wisdom to the next generation—your children.

Heritage Builders®

Helping You Build a Family of Faith

Try These Heritage Builders Resources!

Parents' Guide to the Spiritual Mentoring of Teens

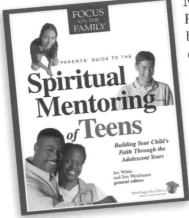

Passing your faith on to your child is like passing the baton in a relay race—it's the most vital part of the contest. In fact, a parent's greatest reward is an adult child who knows, loves, and serves the Lord. That's why the teen years are so critical. They mark the change in the relationship between you and your teen, when your young adult begins to work out his or her faith. This book is a tool that helps you make sense of the change. It gives you practical ways to show your teen how to make faith in God part of everyday life. The *Parents' Guide* is available in hardcover and book-on-cassette— a must-have duo for your home.

Mind Over Media

Set and stick to a family media standard! This topic is of utmost importance to teens—and parents—today! Find out about negative cultural and media influences—especially how to identify and reject them. Discover how to communicate with teens about the pitfalls of popular culture, and how to make a family media standard. *Mind Over Media* is available in video, paperback, and a Dare 2 Dig Deeper booklet entitled, *What's Up With Today's Entertainment?: Separating Trash from Treasure*. Get all three!

My Truth, Your Truth, Whose Truth?

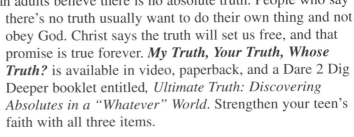

Teens want to know if there's a one <u>real</u> truth. About 75 percent of American adults believe there is no absolute truth. People who say there's no truth usually want to do their own thing and not obey God. Christ says the truth will set us free, and that promise is true forever. *My Truth, Your Truth, Whose Truth?* is available in video, paperback, and a Dare 2 Dig Deeper booklet entitled, *Ultimate Truth: Discovering Absolutes in a "Whatever" World*. Strengthen your teen's faith with all three items.